Advance Praise

"If a small team from Finland can launch a global phenomenon like Angry Birds and get over 5 billion downloads, then you can do it too! Ludovic Bodin's Atomic Scaling is your ultimate playbook for unlocking explosive growth in your business. Get ready to level up, make history, and reach new heights!"

—PETER VESTERBACKA, FORMER MIGHTY EAGLE AT ROVIO, CREATORS OF ANGRY BIRDS

"I am happy to see all these learnings combined in one book to help future entrepreneurs, not just in the games industry but all industries."

—ILKKA PAANANEN, CO-FOUNDER AND CEO AT SUPERCELL

"Atomic Scaling is a game-changing asset that offers effective strategies for achieving exponential growth and success in the digital age."

—ALAIN CROZIER, FORMER CEO (GREATER CHINA) AT MICROSOFT

"*Atomic Scaling is a game-changer, offering groundbreaking insights into the gaming industry that are essential for any entrepreneur looking to succeed in today's increasingly online business landscape.*"

—CHRISTINE COMAFORD, *NEW YORK TIMES* BESTSELLING AUTHOR OF *POWER YOUR TRIBE, SMARTTRIBES* AND *RULES FOR RENEGADES*

"*Ludovic Bodin's Atomic Scaling is a must-read for anyone who underestimates the power of gamers and the gaming industry, providing an insightful framework and invaluable lessons that shed light on how gamers are driving the future of entertainment, technology, and society.*"

—KEVIN LIN, CO-FOUNDER OF TWITCH

"*Ludovic Bodin's Atomic Scaling is a game-changing playbook for gamers and entrepreneurs, empowering them with the principles to unlock unprecedented success in any industry, making it a must-read for those looking to leverage their gaming expertise for exponential growth.*"

—RALF REICHERT, CO-FOUNDER OF ESL

"*A well-written book gives the reader the ability to peek into an author's mind. You do not want to miss the chance to peek into the mind of Ludovic Bodin. In twenty-five years of studying creativity across the world and after interviewing some of the most creative people on the planet, I can honestly say that Ludovic's mind is arguably the sharpest and brightest mind I have had the privilege of learning from. Do not miss this chance to learn from him too.*"

—FREDRIK HÄRÉN, AUTHOR OF *THE IDEA BOOK*

"Atomic Scaling is a breath of fresh air in a world that has gone crazy for startups. In contrast to the Blitzscaling approach that has bred swift but precarious growth, this book lays out the foundations for a leaner and more sustainable way to scale hypergrowth. As a CMO who has gone from the gaming industry to working with startups across SaaS, fintech, consumer, and AI, I've seen the way gaming principles are starting to infiltrate all kinds of startups. Ludovic's book is the most comprehensive analysis I've seen of how this can be applied to every aspect of building long-term, enduring companies."

—OLIVER LO, FORMER VICE PRESIDENT OF
MARKETING AT SEQUOIA CAPITAL

"Atomic Scaling is a must-read for entrepreneurs and industry professionals. Small and independent teams of high talent help us to scale our businesses, tapping into our collective strengths and propelling us to new heights as a united force in the industry!"

—TOUKO TAHKOKALLIO, FORMER GAME DESIGNER (BOOM
BEACH & HAYDAY) AND GAME LEAD AT SUPERCELL

"Games have pioneered technology (3D graphics, new input devices) and business models (free to play, microtransactions) for decades. Ludovic Bodin's Atomic Scaling is a captivating and enlightening journey into the remarkable growth of the gaming industry, offering invaluable lessons for all. It's a call to take gaming seriously and a blueprint for achieving exponential growth in any industry."

—CHARLES HUANG, CO-FOUNDER OF
GUITAR HERO BY ACTIVISION

"This amazing book is loaded with money-making ideas and insights on success. It will make you rich faster than you ever thought possible."

—BRIAN TRACY, SPEAKER AND BESTSELLING AUTHOR OF EAT
THAT FROG!, THE PSYCHOLOGY OF SELLING, AND GOALS

"A must-have playbook for anyone seeking to redefine the rules of the game. Atomic Scaling offers powerful insights from the gaming industry's unprecedented success, providing a roadmap for achieving breakthrough results."

—VERNE HARNISH, FOUNDER OF ENTREPRENEURS'
ORGANIZATION (EO) & SCALING UP

"I was skeptical at first. How can a traditional brick-and-mortar wholesale business like ours apply the lessons from gaming? But our team of almost thirty and I were floored. Ludovic Bodin's Atomic Scaling widened our perspectives and showed us innovative ways of engaging our customers and achieving exponential growth."

—TINA SANTOS, CEO OF SUY SING

"The gaming industry is one of the fastest-growing and most exciting sectors in which to launch a business or build a career. This book is an amazing resource for any entrepreneur looking to understand the transformative power of focused, talented teams. It demonstrates that, with the right approach, small groups can achieve extraordinary things in the gaming industry and beyond."

—JAMES LALONDE, CO-FOUNDER & CO-CEO OF YODO1

"For entrepreneurs hungry to learn from fast-paced, savvy fellow founders, Atomic Scaling is a must read."

—RICH ROBINSON, ENTREPRENEUR-IN-
RESIDENCE AT ANIMOCA BRANDS

"Atomic Scaling by Ludovic Bodin is a compelling and thought-provoking book that illuminates the innovative strategies driving the gaming industry's remarkable growth, and offers valuable lessons for companies seeking to stay ahead of the curve in a rapidly-evolving marketplace."

—SOCRATE LAO, COO OF SOCIETE GENERALE, CHINA

"As Atomic Scaling reveals the success recipe of the gaming industry, we realize it actually presents a working implementation of LEAN Six Sigma, built from first principles to fit that hyperscale, playful, fast paced and data-driven industry. This packed and practical book applies to all industries of the twenty-first century, especially to all these non-manufacturing processes that were still missing their silver bullet toolbox."

—JEROME CLERAMBAULT, DIGITALIZATION EXPERT
AND LEAN SIX SIGMA BLACK BELT, AT AIRBUS

"Ludovic is an insightful person who not only has given me guidelines in how to structure an online business but has also shattered old outdated models of thinking that were blocking our progress. Conversations with Ludovic will revolutionize your paradigm!"

—JASON SHIELDS, FOUNDER AT THE INTEGRATED HUMAN,
3X MASTER WORLD CHAMPION IN BRAZILIAN JIU JITSU

"The Atomic Scaling program from ludovic is literally and figuratively a 'game-changer.' It immersed me and my key managers in the mindset of the gaming industry and opened our consciousness to the possibilities of integrating this into our workflows, particularly in terms of product development and marketing. This is a must-have for any business organization, particularly those who want to enter new markets and expand their reach."

—JAIME NOEL SANTOS, CO-FOUNDER AND PRESIDENT
OF THAMES INTERNATIONAL EDUCATION GROUP

"I love seeing small teams build big things. This book embodies the idea of leverage and provides tactics for leaders looking to do a lot with a little."

—ERIC JORGENSON, CEO OF SCRIBE MEDIA, AUTHOR OF *THE ALMANACK OF NAVAL RAVIKANT* AND *THE ANTHOLOGY OF BALAJI*

"For the future wave of entrepreneurs seeking gaming industry insights, Atomic Scaling is now at your fingertips."

—CHEN QI, CEO OF CENTURY GAMES

"In the advent of AI empowering a single entrepreneur to build a billion-dollar company, Atomic Scaling offers the perfect playbook from the gaming world on how small teams can achieve exponential growth."

—GEORGE GODULA, FOUNDER AND CHAIRMAN OF WEB2ASIA

"I wish I had had this book ten years ago when we founded GetLinks Inc. Good market timing with great operations execution can only get you so far. You still need to make magic and transform your products into a business that can serve the people at scale. And that is where Atomic Scaling comes in."

—DJOANN FAL, CO-FOUNDER OF GETLINKS AND ATLAS VENTURES

Atomic Scaling

ATOMIC SCALING

How Small Teams
Create Huge Growth

LUDOVIC BODIN

HOUNDSTOOTH
PRESS

ATOMIC SCALING
How Small Teams Create Huge Growth

FIRST EDITION

ISBN   978-1-5445-4500-4 *Hardcover*
         978-1-5445-4499-1 *Paperback*
         978-1-5445-4498-4 *Ebook*

For Jiang, Miya, and Anna,
and the wonder of their
unconditional love.

CONTENTS

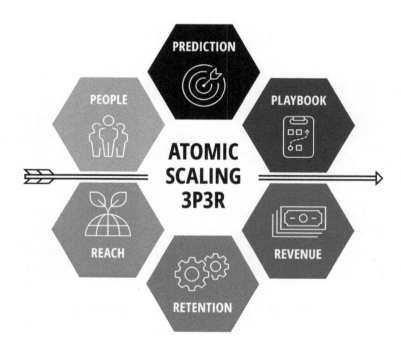

THE ATOMIC SCALING 3P3R FRAMEWORK

1. People: Hire less, empower more.
2. Prediction: Prediction is as important as production.
3. Playbook: Create a finite game and play to win.
4. Revenue: Offer your basic service for free.
5. Reach: Serve the largest total addressable market you can.
6. Retention: Retention is more important than reach or revenue.

QUICK START

Over the last two decades, video game companies have out-performed nearly every industry, yet many still don't take the gaming industry seriously.

Might there be some lessons to learn from an industry producing three times more revenue than Hollywood—and growing?

For example, how can a company from a small country generate twelve billion dollars in revenue in six years—with a team of three hundred people?

How can one product make twenty billion dollars in revenue?

How can a company become the most profitable company per employee—without a boss?

How can products crafted by a few reach a billion-plus people?

How can a company's yearly revenue grow from one billion to fifty billion dollars in just twelve years?

How can a company design an economy that outperforms most governments?

The answer is Atomic Scaling.

For the past twenty years, I have lived, invested, and worked in Europe, Latin America, North America (including Silicon Valley), and China. As a gaming, tech, and AI entrepreneur and investor, I have met many of the world's most successful gaming CEOs. I began to notice they were able to do some things very well that were unheard of or unimaginable in other industries. And they were able to achieve this immense success while making the whole process fun and creating meaning in their work.

I noticed their success followed the same pattern: small teams, exponential growth. You could call this type of growth Atomic Scaling.

They also tend to follow the same principles to achieve this type of growth—principles that happen to be very different from the business growth principles followed by nearly every other industry.

In this book, I share these principles in the form of the 3P3R framework®. It is a navigation system with six elements:

- 3Ps composing your organizational capability: People, Prediction, Playbook
- 3Rs composing your sales funnel: Revenue, Reach, Retention

Atomic Scaling could be particularly relevant to those involved in the software industry, E-commerce, SaaS, EdTech, Fin-Tech, or gaming. Additionally, if you are a business owner, an executive in a large company who recognizes the increasing importance of online business, a government agency seeking new models for SMEs to grow, or an investor, angel, VC, or solopreneur aspiring to the Working from Anywhere lifestyle, then Atomic Scaling may be of interest to you.

As you read this book, I ask only two things of you:

- Please have an open mind.
- Honestly reflect on the way you run your business, what truly matters most to you, and how you can improve your impact on the world.

Now, let's play.

INTRODUCTION

Scale to Serve

EASY ROUND

Here is the introduction in five points:

1. The business world has not typically taken the gaming industry seriously.
2. The gaming industry has crushed all other industries in nearly every metric that matters.
3. The gaming industry has a unique approach to business model, management, and problem-solving that has caused it to crush all other industries. I call this approach Atomic Scaling.
4. Atomic Scaling is the way of the future.
5. No matter what industry you're in, you have a unique opportunity to be an early adopter. This book will show you how.

If you're ready to start applying Atomic Scaling to your business, you can jump to Part One.

If you want to learn more about any of these points, keep reading.

Business is often compared to a game. For many entrepreneurs, founders, or business owners, the game goes something like this:

Wake up in the morning, work as hard as you can for as long as you can, go to bed without really being sure you've accomplished what matters, and wake up the next morning to start all over again.

Meanwhile, time seems to speed up—important personal projects are unfinished, the kids are growing up without you, and you're on the edge of burnout. It feels like nothing you do is ever enough, yet that drive to finally be "enough" is what keeps the cycle going: every morning you get out of bed to try again. Maybe today will be different.

That's not to say life as an entrepreneur isn't exciting. Business is perhaps the most exciting game because it's addictive. But it's also one of the most stressful.

In other words, if business is a game, for many people it's not much fun.

What if you could play a different kind of game?

What if you knew exactly what to focus on each day, enjoyed doing your work, finished up around 3 p.m. or so, spent the rest of the day with the people you care most about, completed personal projects that are meaningful to you, and went to bed (most nights) feeling satisfied, accomplished, and at peace?

What if you weren't just hoping you were doing a good job but *knew* you were doing a good job compared to your business peers because you had the benchmarks to prove it?

What if you were having a visible positive impact on your own life and your family's lives—as well as on your employees, your employees' families, and your customers?

What if you realized you were not just building a company, you were building a community—a community whose members were having an exponentially positive effect on everyone they encountered?

What if the game of business could be more *fun*—without sacrificing profit or meaning?

Many founders and teams play this game every day. In fact, there is one industry that more reliably produces this reality than any other.

The gaming industry.

Before I explain why, let me tell you a little about myself. I started out as a tech and gaming entrepreneur. I was a pioneer in social games and free-to-play games, and I founded and sold a few companies.

I'm also an investor. I've spent the last couple of years traveling around the world, listening to entrepreneurs chase their big dreams and pitch their ideas, and deciding which one I will invest in. Right now, I'm an investor in a gaming company in Silicon Valley, a gaming company in Vancouver, an e-commerce company in Shenzhen, an entertainment company in Beijing, a fan engagement company in Europe, an algo-trading company in Hong Kong, an artificial intelligence company in Paris, a new car company, and a longevity and healthcare company in New York.

I've been blessed with my investments. In 2022, two of my companies became unicorns, meaning that each of them got valued at over $1 billion. One is Chiliz, a sports fan engagement company. The other one is AIG, a live streaming and entertainment company based in Beijing. And I predict at least another company in my portfolio is going to become a unicorn in 2023. So, I'm a lucky investor!

Many people think tech and gaming people are very lucky—and the rich keep getting richer. In many cases, this is true. But it's not just luck.

I began writing this book when COVID-19 hit, when I realized that the gaming industry was likely to do well, but many other industries would suffer as they would be forced to go digital at a faster pace than they could have anticipated.

At the same time, people in traditional industries began to notice that tech and gaming people were doing extremely well through the pandemic, and they began to pay attention to how they were doing so well online. Because most gaming companies were *already* 100 percent online.

Before the pandemic, most traditional industries—including retail, auto, sports, and education—earned only 3-10 percent of their revenue online. That's changing quickly.

During the pandemic, we realized we could work from home.

We realized we could work together productively with digital tools even when we weren't in the same building. We started learning all kinds of things because we had to—we didn't have a choice. All that muscle around innovation, flexibility, and creativity we didn't think we had, we had all along. We just needed to use it.

Now that you know you can grow your business online, ask yourself, post-pandemic, if you want to go back to the old way of doing business or if you're ready to take the red pill (to use an analogy from *The Matrix*) and learn from the tech and gaming industries that are 100 percent online.

The world now knows that 25 percent of the market will move online by 2025, and that number will only continue to grow— for all industries. One of the companies I work with is a German car company, one of the biggest companies in the world. They know if they can't serve customers online by 2025, a quarter of their customers will go to the competition who can.

One of my favorite science-fiction writers, cyberpunk pioneer William Gibson, is commonly quoted as saying, "The future is already here—it's just not very evenly distributed."[1] In terms of business models, tech and video gaming companies are the future.

"The future is already here—it's just not very evenly distributed."

—WILLIAM GIBSON

I wrote *Atomic Scaling* because I want to give back. I want to help all people in all industries create new ways to generate wealth online. That's my mission. I want to share the lessons

I've learned with entrepreneurs, changemakers, founders, executives, and philanthropists who want to positively impact the lives of those they serve and their communities, and I hope I will be able to serve you too.

THE FASTEST WAY FROM ZERO TO A BILLION

Twenty years ago, oil companies and banks were among the most valuable companies worldwide. Then came tech companies, which have generated 80 percent of the world's wealth in the last twenty years. Tech companies now have the largest market cap worldwide.

Twenty years ago, tech companies like Facebook, Google, and Apple held the record for the fastest way to go from zero to a billion, whether in revenue or user base.

Then ten years ago, within tech companies, came gaming companies like Riot Games, Supercell, and Tencent. Now they hold the record for the fastest way to reach a billion in revenue or user base.

In the last decade:

- Riot Games made US$20 billion with one game: League of Legends.
- In five years, Supercell annual revenue has grown from zero to US$2 billion, with fewer than 150 people and only three games: Hay Day, Clash of Clans, and Boom Beach.
- Tencent increased its revenue from US$1 billion in 2008 to US$50 billion in twelve years (that's 50x growth) and became the largest gaming company worldwide.

That's the type of growth experienced by game companies in last ten years.

My friend Bertrand Schmitt is the co-founder of Data.ai (formerly App Annie), the largest analytics and tracking tool for apps worldwide, which tracks the revenue of hundreds of thousands of mobile games and applications. He said the other day that the video game industry is predicted to reach over $300 billion by 2025. A large part will be from mobile games.

If you think your industry will be impacted by artificial intelligence (AI), you know that whoever has the most data has a clear advantage. With more than 2.7 billion gamers in the world in 2020, the gaming industry has a lot of data points. A game like League of Legends alone hosts more than one hundred million players each month. One million people are currently playing as you are reading this. In fact, statistically speaking, at least a third of you reading this are gamers yourselves, even if it means playing a simple game like Candy Crush.

Gaming companies are at the forefront of using AI when it comes to interacting with customers. In fact, they have been at the forefront of AI for the last seventy years, with most AI breakthroughs coming from games like chess, PacMan, the famous Deep Blue vs. Kasparov matches in 1997, and what Kai-Fu Lee called the Sputnik moment of AI with Alpha Go beating the Go game champion.

Because gaming companies are already dealing with hundreds of millions of users and billions of data points, they are already measuring, automating, and winning, thanks to AI.

Gaming, when it comes to making money online, is big, growing, and becoming more powerful.

So how come the world knows so little about gaming?

Would it make sense for you, if you also want to grow online, to learn from the gaming industry?

This is what I am going to share with you in the pages ahead. More people are moving their businesses online now than ever before, and you will be one of them.

While other entertainment services, like the film industry, are falling, gaming is going to grow in the years ahead. It means these business principles will become even more prominent. You have the opportunity to be an early adopter, here and now, and get a competitive advantage. And if you combine the principles in this book with the power of AI, you will have an even stronger advantage.

THE ATOMIC SCALING BLUEPRINT

"Every well-built house started in the form of a definite purpose plus a definite plan in the nature of a set of blueprints."

—NAPOLEON HILL

If you have big dreams as an entrepreneur, business owner, changemaker, or philanthropist, and you're getting exhausted by the "game" of business, you may be wondering how you can compete with the Apples and Amazons of the world.

Finland, the mecca of mobile games worldwide, has a saying: Start Small, Think Big.

This book contains a simple blueprint that allows you to quickly assess where you are in your business, what you are prioritizing, what you may be ignoring, where you need to focus your attention to facilitate growth, and what you can do about it *right now*.

Of course, you don't want just any blueprint to grow your business. For example, one popular approach to business growth is known as *blitzscaling*.

Blitzscaling is (forgive me) a typically American approach. It focuses only on exponential growth: hire as many people as possible, to scale as quickly as possible, to grow as big as possible. A successful example of blitzscaling would be Google, which grew its number of employees from 284 in 2001 to 16,805 employees in 2007—while growing its revenue in the same six years from USD 86 million to USD 16.6 billion. Clearly a success, if we consider Google's current omnipresence on the internet. But outside of Silicon Valley, who can or even wants to hire 16,805 employees in six years?[2]

In contrast to blitzscaling, the blueprint you will find in this book is called Atomic Scaling. Much like atomic power, it allows you to scale exponentially while remaining as small as possible. It focuses on scaling your *impact*, not your size. Atomic Scaling takes a typically European or New Zealander approach: create something beautiful, make it blossom, and become a light for the rest of the world.

Atomic Scaling is the business operating system of the gaming industry developed in the Artificial Intelligence Age, where prediction matters as much as production.

"The sets of lessons we learned in the video games business will be true of a much wider range of industries tomorrow."

—GABE NEWELL, CO-FOUNDER AND CEO OF VALVE

To my knowledge, this business operating system has never been written or shared before, except in pieces here and there. It is the collective wisdom of the game industry. It is who we are and how we do what we do. Success in gaming doesn't happen by accident. Companies like Supercell or Riot have a proven system for achieving success that is a product of the collective wisdom of the gaming industry.

As a business owner, how would you rate your performance in this game? Are you enjoying the gameplay?

We all can choose our own adventure. Let's dream of a new future, and let's make it a future where we can all thrive. Now is the time to do something. Now is the time to get involved.

What do *you* want to scale? The blueprint is in your hands.

It all starts with your People.

Ludovic Bodin

Part 1

THE 3PS: PEOPLE, PREDICTION, AND PLAYBOOK

....

Chapter 1

PEOPLE

"You don't build a business. You build people, and then people build the business."

—ZIG ZIGLAR

Years ago, as a young VC-backed entrepreneur, I was building my third business, and it was growing fast. You may have heard the sales motto ABC—always be closing. Well, VC-backed companies also had a motto: *always be hiring.* As the founder, your job was to always be hiring, and if you didn't have enough money to hire, you just raised more money until you could.

This model was invented in Silicon Valley, where there are more venture capitalists per capita than anywhere else in the world. Generally speaking, this blitzkrieg-type model works well if you move your headquarters to Silicon Valley, raise money from US investors, and become an American company. However, this model is not good for everyone—especially the home countries of non-American entrepreneurs.

It can be challenging for entrepreneurs in Silicon Valley too. As humans, we are not fit to suddenly go from managing a few employees and doing most things ourselves to managing three thousand people. With a blitzscaling model, founders need to significantly upgrade their management skills every three months or so. If you're not able to do that (and most founders aren't), you're likely to be fired and replaced by the VC.

Luckily for me, I was based in Beijing, a city with a comparable talent and investor concentration to Silicon Valley, and my VCs were very supportive. In fact, my lead investor was a European—Niklas Zennstrom, the founder of Skype. Even so, I still needed to always be hiring, and in my case, that meant hiring people not just from China but from all over the world. Our people were moving to China from Poland, Ukraine, Russia, the United States, Canada, and India without speaking the language and without knowing anyone. Culturally for them, it was very challenging to integrate. It was very challenging for us as well.

In gaming, we say that the best people make the best games. So the motto "always be hiring" made sense to us. The new hires always seemed better than the previous ones. Maybe you've been in this situation, where with every new hire, you feel like you're raising the bar for talent, and you believe your next hire is going to be even better than your last hire.

But the truth was that the more people I hired, the less productive the team was.

The more time I spent traveling, raising capital from venture capitalists, and on the phone interviewing people, the less time

I spent with my team. I was also spending a lot of time far away from my family, which made me feel anxious.

I began to feel out of control. I started doubting everything. Every time I came back to the office from a business trip that took two, three, or sometimes five or six weeks, I felt like I was in crisis mode, trying to fix all the things that happened while I was gone.

I began to believe I was not a good manager or a good leader. How could I support my team well if I was not physically there? I had trouble trusting people. Sometimes I even had doubts about my co-founder. Was he a good leader himself? Was he a good manager?

One day I visited Finland to meet a few investors and entrepreneurs in the gaming industry, including Ilkka Paananen, CEO of Supercell, a gaming company you might have heard of. At that time, Supercell was growing fast, but it was not as famous as it is now. Now Supercell is the number one mobile game company, producing mobile games like Clash of Clans, Clash Royale, and Boom Beach, each of which have generated at least $1 billion since their launch. One of them, Clash Royale, has generated $10 billion.

I was with Ilkka in Helsinki, having breakfast downstairs from his office. I was explaining that I was having a difficult time: because I was spending so much time interviewing and traveling, and not spending enough time with my team, I felt they were losing direction and not being very efficient.

"Why don't you stop hiring and focus more on your existing team?" Ilkka responded calmly.

At first, I did not find this to be helpful advice. I explained to him that I had twenty-five team members for one game, and we needed at least sixty because there were many more features and cool things we wanted to bring to the game.

Ilkka told me Clash of Clans was developed by a team of five to six people, and it was released after six months of development. Three months later, it was the highest-grossing game in the US. By 2013, it was the most profitable game in the world. Today it only takes twenty to thirty people to manage it. Yet I thought I needed at least sixty people for my game.

Then Ilkka told me something that changed my entrepreneurial life forever: "The best team indeed makes the best game, but great individuals do not necessarily make a great team."

He said he would rather focus on keeping each team relatively small, like two to five people during development, and focus more of his attention on making the team great rather than constantly hiring new people and growing the size of the team.

This approach had obviously paid off for him, so I tried it for myself. I found that the two principles of keeping teams small plus focusing on team performance were very satisfying. Instead of feeling I could never do enough, I was able to focus on doing more with what I had. Plus, it was a lot more fun to exchange ideas with a few engaged people than have a sterile ten-person meeting where half the people don't even participate.

If you are in a leadership position, hiring and managing your people can feel like an emotional roller coaster. Maybe you don't have enough resources to hire the talent you want. Maybe you don't have enough people on your team to do the job. Maybe you cannot keep the right people in the organization; people are constantly churning. Maybe you have hired the people with the skills your company needs, you have a logical plan to follow, and yet your people still don't get the job done.

You're not alone. Many leaders have felt the same way, including me. The solution is likely the *opposite* of what you have heard.

Instead of "always be hiring," *keep your teams small—and focus on team performance rather than individual talent.*

Beginning with this chapter, we'll be talking about the 3Ps, which form your organizational capability: People, Prediction, and Playbook. Out of the 3Ps, People are the most important. Even with great prediction and a great playbook, your people will make or break a great idea.

Every investor in the world would tell you something like the following: "I invest in extraordinary people" or "I invest in good people doing great things."

But great people don't build great things. Great people *together* make great things.

Many people have the excellent skills required to make great products and businesses. Many studios worldwide—including two gaming companies in Israel and the Middle East which I recently passed on investing—have great people working on great ideas.

The magic, truth be told, is not in the skill set. The magic is in the *combination* of those skills together, with the right skills prioritized at the right time.

In this chapter, you will learn the People principles the top gaming companies have used to scale their profits while staying as small as possible for as long as possible:

- Think with both sides of your brain.
- Stay as small as possible.
- Focus on team performance rather than employee performance.
- Focus on magical pairs.
- Hire EPIC employees.

They know what Richard Branson, founder of Virgin, is famous for saying: "A company is no more than a group of people."

How do you increase your company performance?

It's all about the people.

THINK WITH BOTH SIDES OF YOUR BRAIN

Since we're talking about people, let's begin with the founder or leader of your company. In other words, let's begin with you.

The most important skill for a founder or leader is to be able to *think with both sides of their brain.* Over the years, I have noticed that right-brain storytelling skills *and* left-brain analytical skills truly matter for those in a leadership role.

Gaming is one industry that leverages all brain faculties, both the left-brain skills of the engineers and the right-brain skills of the artists. Gaming is a rare mix of both the left brain and right brain, and that's precisely its powerful innovation.

In particular, gaming team members excel at going back and forth between the right brain and the left brain. Think of the windshield wipers of your car. The left brain is all about logic, while the right is about emotion.

First, the right brain: storytelling skills are essential for leaders because if you can tell a compelling story, you can trigger the right emotional state and the motivation to execute.[3]

Emotions put great ideas into motion. The English word "emotion" is derived from the Latin word *emovere*, which means to move or set in motion.[4] Emotions help us to take action, to survive, to surpass ourselves, to make decisions, to understand others, and to allow other people to understand us.

Without emotion, an idea is not much more than a task on a checklist, a reminder message on Discord or Slack, a project management card on Trello, ClickUp, or Monday.com. Great ideas do not trigger action; emotions do.

A good storyteller has the unique gifts of attracting people to their cause, increasing the level of creativity of people on the task, and building a better understanding of the why. It ultimately leads to better engagement, more robust execution, and delivery on the how and what.

In short, emotion gets the job done, and often in a way that exceeds expectations—in a delightful moment of pure creativity showing the genius of its maker.

Igniting emotion results in extraordinary development and increases your odds of success. On the contrary, expecting a job to be done because the boss says so usually leads to uninspired and pale results—if they're even completed.

Imagine you are a product leader in a game company, and you come to pitch an idea or a feature to an artist or a developer. You tell them, "I did an in-depth analysis of current top-downloading games for hyper-casual, grossing for the core to mid-core with IAP.

"They have excellent retention and low CPI. They all have multiple features that we don't have yet, and we are going to have those now, so we also are going to have fantastic retention and CPI."

How excited do you think the artist is going to be about implementing your recommendations?

Your report may be factual and even compelling, but it is not a story. It triggers neither enthusiasm nor further great ideas.

Worse, facts alone may unintentionally cause resistance from your team, as they can feel like they're on a treadmill, trudging through a succession of uninspired tasks usually poorly fitting what is actually needed, coupled with inadequate specifications.

And for anyone who has been in the gaming industry long enough, it triggers a feeling that crunch time is coming and may never end.

A list of features alone has never made a great game.

A better way to motivate your team would be to couple that data with a story like the following:

"I am grateful every day to be working in this industry. Games saved my life and helped me to become who I am. Every time I would feel down, angry, or confused, I would play a game that put me in a flow state—where the notion of time and space disappeared. Magically, as I played, my emotional state would reset to a positive one.

"I would not only feel intensely focused but also connected. I would feel in control, able to overcome any task, even detect patterns and predict my next moves. That sense of mastery— you may know the feeling. Not only did that experience bring happiness, it became my calling to use the skills I have to create games that will help others to reach that flow state.

"I know precisely what that feeling is and what actions lead to it. And that's why [segue into data report]..."

As iconic investor Fabrice Grinda says, "As the founder or leader, your passion, your dedication, and the connection between your story and your company are very compelling—not just to your team members, but to investors as well."[5]

At the same time, extraordinary storytelling skills alone are not sufficient to help a team become successful. Even if you can trigger the right emotion and motivation to act, the team still may not know what the product should look like, or what to do next.

You still need the ability to organize and prioritize, which is the job of the left brain. You need to balance your storytelling with an analytical view and learn how to get the team to execute well on a vision, in the proper order, and in an agile way.

We will talk much more about this ability in the Prediction chapter. In fact, for every step in the 3P3R framework, you will need to think with both sides of your brain, and shift easily and repeatedly between the story and the data.

STAY AS SMALL AS POSSIBLE

Most business owners know that people typically make up the highest percentage of a company's overhead. In fact, for tech and creative companies, people are often at least 40—and sometimes up to 80—percent of overall company spending. Human resources are the primary resource.

To become a high-performance organization, you need to have not only exponential revenue growth but *linear* cost growth. If your main cost is employees, Atomic Scaling means accelerating revenue growth faster than your number of hires. That's why putting hiring off for as long as possible, rather than building up a large team as quickly as possible, is one of the core principles.

In fact, the most profitable companies per head are gaming companies like Valve and Supercell, not Apple.

Hiring fewer people to do more may sound logical for profitability, but gaming companies like Valve and Supercell fundamentally believe that small teams are also significantly more productive.

A small team means fewer meetings, fewer management layers, and greater space for creativity.

Yet if the team underperforms, a lot of people think (like I did), *Maybe it's because we're understaffed. We need to increase the size of the team.*

The first thing Ilkka does when a team underperforms is to look at how he can *reduce* the size of the team, not necessarily by firing people but by adjusting the team dynamic to allow some individuals to go to another team or project. Most of the time that solves the problem.

Just because a company is growing in revenue and hiring a lot of people does not necessarily mean it's a high-performance organization. It may just be a company with a lot of employees.

Consider your own experience. What kind of company do you believe is more efficiently productive: a large company with thousands of employees and managers, managers of managers, directors, and senior vice presidents—or a small company?

A small team also helps to keep the entrepreneurial spirit alive. It's much fun to manage a team of three, thirty, or even three hundred people versus the thousands many entrepreneurs believe they must hire. Also, if you want to regularly connect with your teammates beyond work, as "trillion-dollar coach" Bill Campbell recommends, smaller teams make it more likely you'll not only remember everyone's names, but the names of their partners and kids, and what they enjoy doing.[6]

CASE STUDY: SUPERCELL

Imagine you started a company with a few friends, and for five years, you did everything you could to keep the headcount from growing—yet you grew the company to 150 people and generated $2 billion in annual revenue.

That's the story of Ilkka Paananen, co-founder of Supercell. When he and a few friends started the company, he had one motto: Supercell! Remain as small as possible as long as possible. That was the number-one constraint.

Five years later, with annual revenue of $2 billion and a profit of more than $0.5 billion, he had created one of the most profitable companies per head in the entire world.

Before starting Supercell, Ilkka and his co-founder, Mikko Kodisoja, founded a company called Sumea, which was bought by an American company called Digital Chocolate. Ilkka was Sumea's only non-developer and non-artist. He was tasked with sales. Since the other founders thought that the sales guy needed to have a title with maximum credibility, they decided to make Ilkka the CEO despite him having zero relevant work experience.

After Digital Chocolate bought Sumea, they grew to hundreds of employees, which was seen as a success.

But this growth was a drain on their income, as they added in more and more controlling processes and management layers. The more people the company hired, the less productive they became.

Some of the well-intended processes led to unfortunate

outcomes, such as people spending more time preparing presentations for management than doing real work like developing great games. Ultimately, after six years, Ilkka and Mikko decided to leave the company. They had had enough of it.

They encountered the famous Netflix memo on culture, which influenced many tech executives at the time. Sheryl Sandberg—back then the COO at Facebook—and many others say it was the most influential document shared in the last ten years. Ilkka and Mikko were also inspired by it, and they decided that maybe it was time to start a new company. But this time, they wanted to do it differently. They would put the game teams at the front and center of the company and put a lot more effort into team and culture than process and management.

One of their fundamental ideas was that Supercell would be made of small, independent teams, trusted to work together in the pursuit of a common dream of making great games.

That's where the name "Supercell" comes from. Each team independently trusts each other, works together, and is managed like a Formula One team with a "magical pair" at its center (for more on magical pairs, see the section later in this chapter).

On the tenth anniversary of the company, Ilkka shared his ten learnings. One key learning was to *stay as small as possible.*

In "10 Learnings in 10 Years," Ilkka explains the surprising benefits of having small teams. "Often, at least in our case, small teams can do better work and higher quality than bigger teams. Having fewer people in a team forces it to focus on what matters and what brings the whole company's biggest impact. On the contrary, having larger teams often leads to 'inventing' work that only looks useful.

The constraint theory was a management principle I was well aware of, and yet I never thought of putting this focus at the center of my company strategy."

Ilkka said, "We have also learned that growing teams prematurely increases complexity and makes changing direction much harder. We have a few cases where we had to make the team smaller to get back on track, and in many cases, that has worked out."

As Ilkka says, "Ten years in, all Supercellians still fit neatly into one frame!"[7]

FOCUS ON TEAM PERFORMANCE, NOT INDIVIDUAL TALENT

According to Ilkka, Supercell realized that having high-performing *teams* was more important than a team of high performers.

What's the difference, and why does it matter? Both may appear to be "high performing," but the different focus drives two different outcomes.

Similar to soccer, basketball, or Formula One racing, the game is won by teams, not superstars.

"No matter how brilliant your mind or strategy, if you're playing a solo game, you'll always lose out to a team."

—REID HOFFMAN, *THE START-UP OF YOU*

If you're trying to solve the organization performance equation, you have two variables. The first variable is the quality of the individual you hire, and the second is team performance.

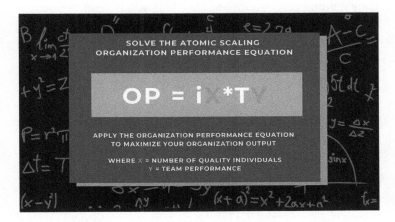

Do your best at hiring the best individuals, but more importantly, get better at what matters most: team performance. If your organization is struggling with performance, rather than constantly looking for a solution outside of the organization, such as hiring new people, look within at how you can improve and maximize your team performance.

So how can a company improve their teams' performance?

One word: trust.

In his well-known example, Simon Sinek notes that not many organizations can boast of measuring trust more than the Navy.[8]

During his work with the Navy SEALs, Sinek asked how they chose who becomes part of their most elite teams—those who are the best of the best.

In response, they drew a graph: on the y-axis, they wrote the word *performance*, and on the x-axis, they wrote the word *trust*.

They defined performance as the skills you had on the battle-field, and trust as the kind of person you were off the battlefield.

According to Sinek, here's how they defined trust: "I trust you with my life, but do I trust you with my money and my wife?"

When it came to the most elite teams, they obviously wanted the people who scored high on performance and high on trust, and they obviously did not want someone who scored low on performance and low on trust.

Where it gets interesting is who they would choose when the choice wasn't obvious.

Sinek said that the Navy SEALs would rather have a medium performer with high trust, and sometimes even a low performer with high trust, over a high performer with low trust—because they knew the high performer with low trust was toxic.

Which would you choose?

Here is Sinek's point: The United States Navy is one of the highest-performing organizations on the planet, and trust is more important to them than performance. Yet in business, we have no metrics to measure trust and many metrics to measure performance. As a result, we reward the toxic leaders and team members, and end up destroying our organizations in the long term.[9]

One company I invested in had exactly this problem. They hired a sales team member who seemed to be a top performer with a strong network. He was also incredibly toxic—to the point where it was damaging the whole company because nobody wanted to work with him. Ultimately, the company discovered he was *not* a top performer, in addition to being toxic, and he got fired. But it took the company six months to finally make this decision, causing a lot of damage to their existing team in the meantime.

In Chapter 6, we're going to focus on the importance of *retention*. Just as People is the important P of the 3Ps, Retention is the most important R of the 3Rs. Most people know it is far cheaper to retain and upsell existing customers than to acquire new customers.

What many people forget is the same is true for employees: it is far cheaper to retain an existing employee than to hire and train a new employee. Retention begins with your own team.

Even big companies are often not very good at retaining their people, as we've seen clearly in what is often called the Great Resignation. In 2021, 47.4 million Americans voluntarily left their jobs.[10] As it turns out, they weren't just resigning; they were upgrading. Most were no longer willing to tolerate jobs, bosses, or coworkers who made their lives miserable.

You may not be familiar with Supercell or Valve, but you've

probably watched movies or shows on Netflix. As mentioned earlier, Supercell's original idea was inspired by Netflix's culture.

Netflix is one of the few companies that doesn't reward people based on performance but rewards people based on how well they exhibit Netflix's values. One of Netflix's core values is "We are what we do." And they really mean it. If you demonstrate the values of Netflix's culture, you get promoted or receive a raise. If you're a jerk, even if you are a top performer, you're fired.

The key to retaining your employees is to *create a culture of trust*—and protect that culture at all costs.

In the very near future, companies will no longer be able to get away with hiring toxic, untrustworthy employees, whether they are high performing or not.

For now, you can be ahead of the curve and ask yourself the following questions:

- What if you cared as much about retaining your top employees as you do about retaining your top customers?
- How would your onboarding, training, and other HR practices change if your employees were just as valuable to you as your customers?

However, the highest-performing game companies don't just hire trustworthy individuals. For some, their entire structure is based on trust.

Ilkka Paananen describes himself as the "least powerful CEO

in the world." Because his culture of independent "cells" has complete autonomy regarding the games they create, they can decide to kill a game or continue with it, even if other cells or even leadership disagrees. This method has produced incredibly successful games, including Clash Royale, Boom Beach, and Brawl Stars.

As Ilkka says, "Decisions should be made by the people best equipped to make them. We believe that the more decisions the teams make, the better it is for us. That is for two reasons: Teams are closest to what they do, and therefore, they should be in the best position to decide the best course of action. If teams can decide independently without seeking approval from others, they will execute faster and be happier."[11]

In the following chapter on Prediction, we'll discuss restructuring your company with the reverse power pyramid—which not only increases the trust in your culture, it also happens to increase your prediction power.

FOCUS ON MAGICAL PAIRS

Here is another secret to team performance. According to Ilkka, "One very concrete thing that we have learned about forming new teams is to first put a very tight and well-functioning core team of, say, two to four people together. In fact, we often talk about how it all starts with finding just *two* people who work extremely well together. There is complete trust, they can complete each other's sentences, and at the same time they bring different perspectives and make each other better."[12]

Supercell calls them *magical pairs*. The result of these two brains working together is exponentially better than one or its sum.

Think of magical pairs as the mechanic and the driver in Formula One racing. In rally racing or pair programming, it would be the pilot and co-pilot. The fast brain and the slow brain.

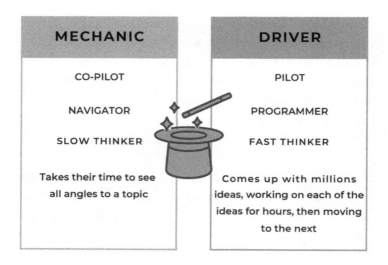

MECHANIC	DRIVER
CO-PILOT	PILOT
NAVIGATOR	PROGRAMMER
SLOW THINKER	FAST THINKER
Takes their time to see all angles to a topic	Comes up with millions ideas, working on each of the ideas for hours, then moving to the next

Here are some more detailed observations about magical pairs from Joakim Achrén—a gaming industry expert from Helsinki, Finland, who previously served as the Director of Analytics at Supercell and co-founded Next Games—concerning the best work he observed on games like Hay Day, Clash of Clans, and Walking Dead: No Man's Land:

> I'd think about two individuals crafting the shape, the form, and the final outline of the game. They'd continuously work together to revise and iterate each other's thoughts, aiming to get to the root of the matter, then expanding outwards and always wanting

to see each problem from every angle. They were comprehensively challenging these thoughts, giving feedback to each other, building knowledge, and building the game.

Why magical pairs? Because, in my opinion, the game design is more likely to become magical if two people are working on the design instead of one.

Here's an example of the magical pair.

Two people walk into a meeting room. They stand in front of a large whiteboard, and a discussion happens. One starts writing things down on the whiteboard, outlining three items. Each of these items represents a problem area within the game design.

This discussion and whiteboard work continues for two and a half hours. After the meeting, both individuals have follow-up tasks to take care of. The following day, these two people meet again and continue their work to solve the existing and new problem areas.

These and some very similar situations were the ways I experienced the concept of "magical pairs" at work. They'd work together, bouncing ideas off and getting feedback from each other, but they'd then continue with singled-out tasks on their own.

Some detailed observations from two designers working on a game:

Magical pairs complement each other. The first one is a *slow thinker*, who takes their time to see all angles to a topic and then finally puts it to paper. At the same time, the second one, who is a *quick thinker*, comes up with millions of ideas, works on each of the ideas for hours, and then moves to the next.

Magical pairs debate and iterate. The individuals will disagree on some fundamental elements and probably get a little mad in these situations. They'll accidentally step on each other's toes. But they'll also come up with amazing ideas that exceed what either of them could do on their own.

Magical pairs work together effectively. They keep notes, preferably in one place such as Google Docs. They have decided what to do when they disagree on something. Their work is effective since they've decided who's going to do what before they get into the work.[13]

Magical pairs create an atmosphere that supports creativity, where there is no dumb idea. This takes a special connection based on trust. As you have probably already discovered, if you share an idea with someone and they respond, "Why are you wasting my time with this stupid idea?" that shuts down creativity, and the project is pretty much over. Neuroscience and business consultant Christine Comaford conveys it this way in her book *SmartTribes*: it puts us in our Critter State instead of our Smart State.[14]

For that reason, this notion of the magical pair is a fundamental investment concept for me. When I consider investing in a company, I look for the magical pair, both in terms of complementary skills and in terms of synergy.

For example, I was introduced to an Israeli gaming and analytics company that appeared very strong on paper. When I heard they were raising money, I was certain I was going to invest in them. Individually, both founders looked really strong and very experienced, but I soon saw that as a team, they were working against each other. Every time one of them would say something, the other would cut them down.

I knew right away it would not work long term. I decided not to invest in them, and sure enough, the company soon shut down.

As Ilkka says, "Once you have a solid core—a magical pair—it is way easier to add people and grow the team. But if you don't yet have a magical pair—do not add new people to the team!"[15]

HIRE EPIC EMPLOYEES

Staying as small as possible does not mean that you stop hiring. You just do it very slowly. The quality of your employees is now more important than ever. As Ilkka puts it, "When thinking about whether you should hire someone or not, try to imagine the average quality level of the people at your company. Then ask yourself whether the new hire would increase that average or not. Only hire if the average will increase."

Remember Simon Sinek's insight about how destructive toxic employees can be. The good news is that hiring the right people can have the opposite effect: it can make your team exponentially more productive. According to a Supercellian (a team member at Supercell), "Working with great people makes everything better. If the team is passionate about their game and knows what they're doing, it will make everything so much easier."[16]

How do you put everything together and hire the right employees *and* create a quality culture? You can use the EPIC framework, where EPIC stands for Employees, Profit, Impact, and Cost.

EMPLOYEES: FOCUS ON USERS SERVED PER EMPLOYEE, NOT TOTAL NUMBER OF EMPLOYEES

As mentioned earlier, if you're following the motto "always be hiring," you're creating a monster nobody wants to be a part of—maybe including you, the founder. If you've ever asked yourself, "Why do the rich get richer? How have tech and gaming companies created so much wealth in the last twenty years?", the answer is their companies are optimized for their employees to serve tons of users. "Tons of users" in the gaming industry means 100,000 to 300,000 users per day per employee.

Instead of "always be hiring," the motto of most gaming companies is "serve a billion users." Instead of asking how many employees they have or should have, they ask, "How many users can I serve per employee?" If you need a billion employees to serve a billion users, that would be horrible in terms of performance or efficiency. That wouldn't even be an efficient government or country. But if you have 300 employees serving a billion people—wow! That means each of your employees serves slightly less than 400,000 people. That's a lot more people served per employee than even Microsoft or Apple.

If you want to hire more people for each new customer you sign, you're not on your way to Atomic Scaling. A better question to ask is, "How many people am I now serving daily?" Or even better, "How many people per employee am I currently serving?"

Valve Corporation, a gaming company whose games include Dota and Counter-Strike, has 62 million daily active users. That means they serve 62 million people every day on the Steam platform, which is their own PC gaming platform. They have 360 employees, most of them in the Seattle area.

On average, Valve has 17 million people concurrently (i.e. online at the same time) on their platform per day; at their peak, they have 25 million people concurrently. With 360 employees, that's 47,000 people served concurrently per Valve employee and 170,000 customers served per employee *per day*.

Again, the reason tech and gaming companies do so well is because they are optimized to serve tons of users without having to hire tons of people. Today, Supercell has 250 million daily active users with only 420 employees. That's three times the number of users served per day per employee at Valve.

You may be wondering, *How can I increase my users per employee to that scale?* The two keys are (1) to remain as small as possible, as we discussed in the previous section, and (2) to automate as much as possible.

When your company is facing a problem, instead of instantly hiring someone new to solve the problem, what if your company asked, "How can we fix the problem with an automated solution?" That's what companies like Valve and Supercell are very good at doing, and ten to twenty years from now, more processes will be automated. We'll focus more on automation in Chapter 3 when we discuss your company's playbook.

For now, it's enough to know that bigger is not always better. Give up the vanity metrics of "always be hiring" and instead focus on increasing the number of customers served per employee.

PROFIT: SCALE YOUR PROFIT FASTER THAN REVENUE OR NEED FOR NEW EMPLOYEES

High-performance organizations scale their results and profit faster than their need for new employees. Profit, at some point, should also scale way faster than revenue so that every new customer produces almost 100 percent profit.

ATOMIC SCALING EXPONENTIAL

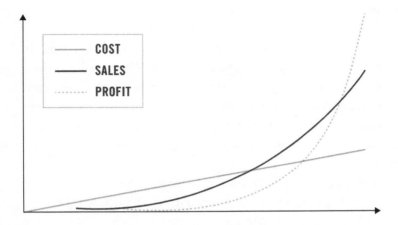

Rather than measuring revenue goals alone, adopt this new metric of scaling profit faster than revenue. Ultimately, the way to scale your profit faster than revenue is to follow the 3P3R framework, so if you want to learn more about how to do this for your business, keep reading!

IMPACT: CLARIFY YOUR COMPANY'S CAUSE

The best people don't join a company for a paycheck (even if it's 2.5 times higher than any other company; see the next section on Cost). The best people join a cause they believe in and have fun being part of. They want to be part of a company where they can feel they can have an impact, or experience what Microsoft's mission statement calls *empowerment.*

If you're not clear about your cause, but your competitor is, here's what will happen. Your competitor will go on LinkedIn, see that you have a lot of talented employees, and offer to pay them two or three times more than what you're paying. (It's pretty easy to figure out how much any one employee is earning right now.)

To prevent employees from being tempted by money alone, focus on the impact your employees will have. Your impact, or cause, can simply be the mission of your company. Your mission can be a meaningful cause for your people if they can relate with your customers, want to serve your customers, and may even fit the profile of your ideal customers.

In gaming, we often use the term "the suit." The suit is typically the guy in a tie, maybe fifty years old and a bit overweight, from business school. He doesn't like to play games himself, but he is highly paid in the gaming industry. On the other side are "the geeks," who like playing games and can relate to customers. The suits are usually the bosses, which is very painful for the geeks.

If you really want to outperform your competition from a People point of view, your people need to be able to relate to the customers—not just have the right business skills or development skills or artistic skills. They have to really *want* to serve your customers. In that way, your mission becomes their cause.

Among the best gaming companies I've seen is a company called Razer, which manufactures mouses and keyboards. Their founder Min-Liang Tan was an investor in my gaming company. When you visit their office, the first thing you notice is that they all seem to be part of a tribe. They all have similar hairstyles, beards, tattoos, and clothing, and they all look like their customers. They're all hard-core gamers. They play music as they work. At the same time, they're very professional and very dedicated.

In contrast, if you visit a company like Activision, one of the two largest US companies in the gaming industry, you feel like you're at Costco—not exactly the kind of place gamers will relate to the most.

Impact is especially important to younger generations; they don't just want a paycheck. They are smart and know they can go from one paycheck to another. They don't want to join monster corporations that look like Costco and are run by suits—no matter what industry they're in. They want to join a cause. They want to make an impact through their work. They want to care about the people they serve.

So, the question is: What kind of cause is your company serving? What meaningful impact can your employees make in their work? The answer is found in your mission and values, which we will discuss in Chapter 3.

COST: INCREASE COST PER EMPLOYEE AFTER PROFITS SCALE

Ultimately, a company with a team that serves tons of users, generates even more profit, and creates meaningful impact should share that profit with its employees. The result is increasing the *cost* of each employee, but only after you have scaled your profits.

At Valve, 360 people are worth around $17 billion. Most of the employees at Valve are either millionaires or billionaires. Similarly, Supercell's founders and key employees are among the largest tax contributors in Finland. The company is also one of the largest tax contributors.

Another reason companies like Supercell and Valve do so well and serve so many people per day with just a few employees is what Valve co-founder and CEO Gabe Newell calls the 2.5x Valve rule. When Gabe started Valve, he was an employee of Microsoft, and he was doing quite well. But at that time, there was a big movement towards trying to find the lowest-cost English-speaking employees anywhere in the world.

Gabe thought that move was precisely the opposite of what a high-performance organization should do. He believed high-performance organizations should find the best talent in the world and reward them accordingly.

For example, as Gabe explains it, an artist who works on a feature film production in New Zealand might make $200,000 a year. If they came to Valve, Gabe's goal would be for that employee to make at least $500,000 (2.5x) and generate up to $5 million in value for the company. As the employee created more and more value, Valve would split the difference with the employee and go from there.[17]

In the Seattle area, where Valve is headquartered, many of the 350 employees have their own family office to manage the multimillion-dollar enterprises they have accumulated as artists, writers, or developers at Valve over the last ten to twenty years.

In comparison, the top twenty-five software as a service (SaaS) companies generate on average $400,000 in revenue per employee per year, which means it's difficult to pay more than $400,000 per employee per year. The top gaming companies, like Supercell, generate $4 million per year per employee. Even if they pay their employees $1 million per year, they're still netting $3 million per employee, so it's easy for them to pay them two, three, or four times as much as other companies.

If you follow the 2.5x Valve rule, people will stick with you forever because you're literally paying them 2.5 times more, and sometimes five or ten times more, than what they would earn at another company. Even more importantly, if you're following the EPIC framework, you're allowing them to have a meaningful impact they might not have elsewhere, even if another company paid them more.

Notice that you must have the E in EPIC before you can have the P, I, and C. People usually make up the highest part of your overhead, so increasing the number of users per *employee* reduces your total employee cost, which allows your *profits* to scale faster than your need for employees.

With higher profits, you can focus on making an *impact* beyond simply surviving as a business—which draws quality people to join your cause—and share those profits with your people by increasing the *cost* of each employee, which still is far less than the benefit the employee provides to the company.

Meanwhile, your employees are not only able to provide for themselves and the people they care about, but they can also finance an orphanage, contribute tax to their country, and sponsor their favorite team, for example, as Supercellians do. When your employees share in the company's success, they are able to make an impact far greater than the impact they make through their work alone (which is also significant).

EPIC employees truly are the top 0.001 percent, and I think

that's where ultimately everyone should be. That's what Atomic Scaling can do: it's not a win/lose game; it's a game where everyone can win.

GAME ON: PEOPLE

☐ **Think with both sides of your brain.** How might you use storytelling *and* data the next time you're enrolling someone in a task or project?

☐ **Stay as small as possible.** Instead of hiring more people, how might you invest in the people and the culture you have to increase performance and profitability?

☐ **Focus on team performance, not individual talent.** How might you create a culture of trust and accelerate team performance in your company rather than focusing on individual skills or talent alone?

☐ **Focus on magical pairs.** Who are the magical pairs in your company? How might you arrange for them to work together more often if they don't work together already? How might you assemble a team around them?

☐ **Hire EPIC employees.**
- ○ **Employees.** How might you increase the number of customers each employee serves?
- ○ **Profit.** Is your profit scaling higher than your revenue? If not, what one thing might move the needle the fastest?
- ○ **Impact.** What is the mission of your organization? Is it more powerful than compensation to your employees? Do your employees care about your customers—do they want to serve them?
- ○ **Cost.** How might you take one step toward the Valve 2.5x rule in your organization?

Chapter 2

PREDICTION

"Prediction matters as much as production."

—GABE NEWELL, CO-FOUNDER AND CEO OF VALVE

As an investor, I meet a lot of entrepreneurs in the early stages who share beautiful presentation decks that tell a beautiful story about how amazing they are and how amazing they will be.

But when I ask them about their financial projections, they stumble a bit. Then they write down a few numbers on a piece of paper, projecting they will make, for example, $1 million within approximately two years.

This scenario is not very exciting for me.

If a company, even in its early stages, does not have the ability to make clear predictions, that means they are not measuring what they are doing. If they do not measure, they will not be able to improve.

Whenever these entrepreneurs face a challenge, they will just come up with a new story.

In the start-up world, this is called a pivot. It's fine to pivot from time to time, even multiple times, if you're actually using data to create and measure a hypothesis and attempting to improve based on that data.

But if you pivot because you spent six months developing an untested story, that's not a good reason to pivot. You likely didn't have enough touchpoints with your customers, or enough ways to actually measure what works and what doesn't.

As discussed in the previous chapter, founders must be able to think with both sides of their brain. They must be storytellers *and* data driven.

Here's a secret from Valve co-founder and CEO Gabe Newell and the gaming industry as a whole: Prediction is as important as production.

Prediction is power. In fact, it's a superpower—not just for the gaming industry, but for every industry.

In Part Two, we will go into more detail about how gaming companies specifically use prediction for revenue, reach, and retention. But for now, just know that if you want to experience more peace as an entrepreneur, you need to get better at prediction.

In this chapter, you will learn about the importance of making good predictions, the difference between prediction and Prophecy, and a simple three-step model for prediction you can use in any industry.

PREDICTION IS AS IMPORTANT AS PRODUCTION

"The iteration of hypothesis, changes, and measurement will make you better at a faster rate than anything else we have seen," says Gabe Newell. If you start using AI, you will improve even faster.

And gaming companies happen to be really good at this.

"The iteration of hypothesis, changes, and measurement will make you better at a faster rate than anything else we have seen."

—GABE NEWELL

Like many other industries, gaming companies are constantly working on forecasting the future, and they do it with access to a large set of data, a clear funnel coupled with a set of hypotheses and benchmarks, and an ability to measure constantly.

They forecast everything from the genre they choose to develop to the art style they choose, the features they prioritize, and the revenue they anticipate from a specific sale or event.

Some forecasts are based on advanced statistical data analysis, some are based on industry benchmarks and past precedents, and others are based on gut feeling. Whatever method you use, the more accurate your forecasting is, the more effective your strategies and project plans will be.

Business forecasting provides a key competitive advantage for any industry. Every product or service you offer should involve collecting data and making predictions based on that data.

For example, the main strength of luxury business LVMH, which includes brands such as Louis Vuitton and Givenchy, is its ability to predict at every level of production—from their ability to predict whether the skin of the cow they buy will produce a fine bag, to exactly how many pieces to produce at Christmas to have virtually zero waste in their supply chain. When they produce 200 Louis Vuitton bags, they know how quickly these bags will sell. If they need 200, they don't produce 202 or 198.

This level of detail is important because the less discrepancy there is between your prediction and what you produce and ultimately sell, the higher your margin. In the case of luxury businesses, they do not simply discount the bags they don't sell, because that will devalue the brand. Instead, they destroy them, which means if they produce more than what they sell, not only will they have lost their production costs, they have the additional cost of destroying what they produced.

The same is true for any industry whose products have an expiration date. If you own a grocery business, the less discrepancy between your prediction of what you will sell and what you actually buy from your suppliers, the higher your margin.

Prediction is also how you will destroy your competition. If you put two supermarkets next to each other, where Supermarket A is good at predicting exactly what it needs to sell and Supermarket B is throwing food away every day, you can be sure that Supermarket B is going to be out of business pretty quickly.

If you're beginning to get worried about your own ability to measure and predict, you are not alone. Most companies are not very good at it.

If I've convinced you that prediction is as important as production, the first step is to make sure those who are best able to predict are empowered to predict. Like most top gaming companies have already done, you need to return the power of prediction to your people.

BRING THE POWER OF PREDICTION TO THE PEOPLE

Once upon a time, when the first factories were created, leaders predicted and the masses produced. Workers were expected to do what they were told.

This way of working is not natural for humanity. Most people are craftspeople; they prefer to use their brain and their hands to solve problems. Being hired not to think and to simply execute what the boss said can be exhausting.

Remember, prediction equals power. During the Industrial Revolution, we removed this power from employees, and it's time to give it back. One way to do that is through a reverse pyramid of power.

CASE STUDY: SUPERCELL

Ilkka Paananen, founder of Supercell, thinks of himself as the world's least powerful CEO. Supercell is a company built around the principle of staying as small as possible as long as possible, made up of small independent teams trusted to work together. (See Chapter 1.)

At Supercell, the boss doesn't decide what the team is going to work on; the team decides what the team is going to work on. They reverse the pyramid of power.

Ilkka noticed over the years that nearly every popular Supercell game had one thing in common: senior leadership had nothing to do with them. In fact, in the case of the most successful game at Supercell, Clash of Clans, leadership was against the game for many, many weeks and months, thinking the game didn't have potential. The team thought differently and continued working on it. A team of five to seven people made Clash of Clans, a team of about twenty people maintain it now, and the game has generated over $7 billion for Supercell.

So Ilkka and the founders of Supercell began to wonder if these games succeeded not because of leadership, but in spite of it.

They started to wonder, what if the creators of the games owned the vision of the game? What if they turned the power structure upside down? There would be no central process, no central control, no approval process for which game you should work on and which game should be killed. Supercell replaced control with trust.

THE PYRAMID MODEL

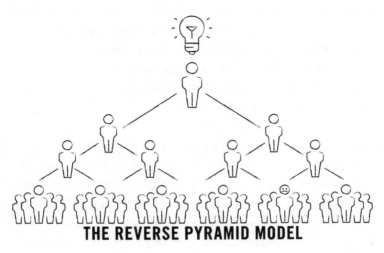

THE REVERSE PYRAMID MODEL

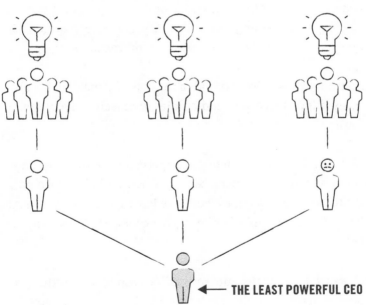

THE LEAST POWERFUL CEO

Those who are the closest to the game and the players of the game know the best thing to do for their game, not the CEO or the founders. The better the game makers are, the better decisions they make. The more decisions they make, the fewer decisions the CEO makes—and the better it is for everyone. That's why Ilkka says his ambition as the founder of Supercell is to be the least powerful CEO.

To give you an idea of what this looks like in practice, Ilkka was leaving Finland for a business trip in San Francisco while his team was continuing to develop a game that had been in beta for six months. When he landed in San Francisco, he saw a message from the team posted to the game's community forum, saying they had decided to cancel the game. You might think, *Wow, after all that time and money spent developing the game and building the community—shouldn't they have at least asked Ilkka for approval before they announced it to the community?*

Instead, Ilkka was very proud of the team for making this obviously difficult decision and holding themselves accountable for it.

"For me, the best moments at Supercell have been the ones where something amazing has happened, and I have had nothing to do with it and have been the last to hear about it," says Ilkka.[18] People think that he is joking when he says that, but he is not.

One day, I was at the Supercell office around 3:30 in the afternoon when Ilkka walked by and said, "Hey, Ludovic. How are you doing? The school day is over, and I'm going to pick up my kids." He was very relaxed about it, and meanwhile, the company was making tons of money, and Ilkka himself is one of the largest tax contributors in his country.

So what *does* Ilkka do? Everything he does is focused on team performance. Now that he doesn't have to make decisions about which game to launch or which feature to include, he has a lot more time to focus on what matters.

> Here is how Supercellians talk about the value of trust and what it means to them:People are more capable than most companies/ cultures allow them to be.

> Most companies are built with hierarchies, processes, and cultures that may teach people but don't let them contribute to their max capacity.

> Supercell has demonstrated that people can deliver incredible achievements when removing approvals, processes, hierarchies, and bureaucracies. That's fundamentally why Supercell has five-hit games that have been played by more than a billion unique players, creating experiences remembered for a long time.[19]

If you want to begin reversing the pyramid of power in your organization and empowering your people to make more decisions on their own, remember that it will not work if you have not already invested in top talent, as we discussed in the People chapter. You must be confident your team is competent enough to do what they need to do.

"My ambition is to be the least powerful CEO."
—ILKKA PAANANEN, CEO AND CO-FOUNDER OF SUPERCELL

Once you are confident in your team, you can begin a transition period where you gradually begin shifting decision-making responsibilities to them. Now the goal is to help them become confident in themselves.

Obviously, there will be a transition period where your team will still ask you lots of questions. To help them make the shift, you need to recognize the question behind the question. When they come to you with a question, what are they really looking for?

You can think of these questions behind the questions as the three A's. Are they looking for *Appraisal*, *Approval*, or *Additional clarification*?

If one of your team members is looking for *appraisal*, they're not necessarily looking for your opinion; they're looking to be evaluated. They want to know if they are doing a good job. Richard Branson, the founder of Virgin, has a famous quote that I like: "People are no different from flowers. If you water flowers, they will flourish." Praise is the water that allows people to flourish.

Praise is a critical leadership attribute. So if someone comes to you and you can tell they have already spent hours trying to figure out the best thing to do, and you detect they do not need your permission or additional clarification, they don't really need your opinion. If they are looking for appraisal, do what Richard Branson is amazing at and make your people flourish with the water of praise.

On the other hand, when some people come to you with a question, they might be looking for your *approval*, or your permission. Ask yourself, do they really need your approval for this decision? Is the decision trivial or nontrivial?

In business forecasting, to decide if something is trivial or nontrivial, we use a framework called the *asteroid framework*. Imagine an asteroid is hurtling toward earth, and with every minute, the likelihood of its potential impact is growing and growing. Similarly, is the impact of the decision before you getting bigger and bigger, and is the rate of change accelerating, like an asteroid? If so, it's most likely a non-trivial decision that does need your approval.

But if it's not, maybe it's a trivial decision. If it's a trivial decision, let the person know they don't need to ask your permission for decisions like this. And then water them with praise.

The third A is *additional clarification*. If people often come to you for additional clarification, you might ask yourself, *Do we have a clear vision of what we're doing? Is our value system clear for everyone?* We'll talk more about that in the next chapter on Playbook.

If you're considering reversing the pyramid of power at your organization, you might be wondering, *If I don't make the project decisions anymore, what exactly will I do as the leader?* Don't worry; you will still have plenty to do! In the reverse pyramid structure, the leaders play the very, very important role of casting the vision and building the culture. This is where inspirational leadership becomes very important.

Leadership at Supercell has a lot more time than most companies to focus on things that matter, and as we learned in the previous chapter, what matters most for these leaders is team performance. Since they're not weighed down with all those detailed decisions, they can walk around the office and see how teams are actually performing, and come up with adjustments to increase team performance.

Your job may be more focused, but it won't necessarily be easier. In fact, leaders who use this reverse power pyramid say it's harder than traditional top-down leadership. The more successful you are, the harder it is *not* to give your opinion about decisions.

Ilkka, for example, says it's a constant challenge. Sometimes he believes a team is on the wrong path and is working on something that doesn't make sense—yet he still encourages his team to move forward. When the fourth team began working on Clash of Clans, it would have been much easier to say, "Okay, we've had three teams trying to do this game Clash of Clans, and you're going to be the fourth. It doesn't make any sense; it's a waste of time. Kill the game and move on to something else."

But if Ilkka or any of the management had done that, Clash of Clans would not have been released, and the company would not have made $10 billion from that single game.

And even when a team does make a poor prediction, at least they will learn from their experience. The most important thing is to maintain this culture of trust and empowerment—which is your job as a leader.

PREDICTION CAN BE LEARNED

Even if you, as the company leader, become comfortable with a reverse power pyramid, it can still be stressful for the team members too. New employees at companies like Valve or Supercell usually leave within six months if they cannot adapt to this management style.

On one hand, not everyone wants independence and responsibility. Some people prefer to do what the boss tells them to do. After all, if they don't make the decisions and things don't work out—well, it's not their fault!

On the other hand, even if team members want the independence and responsibility, they may not know how to make good predictions. They're not alone: most leaders don't know how to make good predictions either!

The good news is that making a prediction can be learned. In fact, prediction is more of a mindset than a talent or a matter of knowing the right information.

Philip Tetlock, Wharton School professor and author of *Superforecasting*, has long been considered an expert in the art and science of prediction. His research has revealed that the best forecasters have something in common: a growth mindset.

You've probably heard of a growth mindset. It's a willingness to learn from past mistakes and continuously update our hypotheses. Our ability to predict can be improved with practice, and a growth mindset fuels our motivation to keep practicing.[20]

Pop quiz: Do you think the companies best at prediction tend to focus on process, or results? In this case, the process would be the method the individual used to make the prediction, and the result would be whether the individual was right or not.

When I ask this question to groups, most answer, "Results." But the answer is process.

Let me explain.

Most of your employees are not trained in prediction. One of the things Twitch—the leading live video streaming service for video games—did very early on was to train their people to make predictions based on past events, not future events (see case study below). If you focus on results too early, your employees will be scared of making the wrong prediction, and then you will get neither process nor results.

Think back to the tests we took in school, where we were graded on whether we had the right answer or the wrong answer. It's very difficult to consistently have the right answer if you've not been trained in how to find the right answer. Once you learn the process, you practice the process, and you get better results as you go. That's why process matters more than results.

"Forecast, measure, revise: it is the surest path to seeing better. To improve is to change."

—PHILIP TETLOCK, AUTHOR OF *SUPERFORECASTING: THE ART AND SCIENCE OF PREDICTION*

The truth is any forecaster who is afraid of being wrong is the one most likely to be wrong in the long run. For example, if you've been good at predictions in the past and you're known as an expert, the longer you publicly state your predictions, the harder it is to change your prediction. Nobody wants to admit they were wrong. Yet the irony is that the longer you make the same prediction out of fear of being wrong, refusing to take new evidence into account, the more likely you are to be proven wrong in the future.

If you receive new information, you should be able to change your prediction. That's why what matters most to top forecasters is not results, but process.

CASE STUDY: TWITCH

Twitch, the leading video live streaming service for video games, is known as a master of prediction. It's a competitor of YouTube and was co-founded many years ago by Justin Kan, Emmett Shear, Michael Seibel, Kyle Vogt, and my friend Kevin Lin.

Twitch TV allows gamers to stream their screen and comment on their game while they are playing. The company has approximately 360 billion hours of video games and was bought by Amazon for close to a billion dollars.

One superpower of Amazon, and more specifically Jeff Bezos, is their capability not only to accurately forecast but to use forecasting to make "high-quality, high-velocity" decisions.

So Twitch adapted the Tetlock principles, Tetlock being the author of *Superforecasting*, and learned how to make a prediction about nearly everything. They developed an internal training program to "create a culture of forecasting and better anticipate the future," according to Twitch data scientist Danny Hernandez.

One of their key learnings, says Hernandez, was to make predictions in terms of *mathematical probabilities*, which forced them to quantify how uncertain they were about future events.

When Twitch began using this method and spreading these principles throughout the company, they first used it to prioritize which features should be added to their services and which should not.

For example, Hernandez wanted to improve Twitch's host mode with an auto-host feature. When he first presented this idea to management, he came with a prediction: "If we build auto host, I'm 70 percent confident that, within eight weeks, 15 percent of our partners (our largest influencers) will be auto-hosting."

This wasn't a guess out of thin air. He had built this prediction, collecting data from streamers and from the lead developer who developed the new feature.

This concrete prediction gave the team confidence in making decisions moving forward, and now auto host is one of Twitch's most popular features for their top streamers. To further illustrate this principle, Hernandez shares an actual conversation between a Twitch manager and an employee:

Employee: "I'll get Project X done this quarter."

Manager: "How surprised would you be if it wasn't done by the end of the quarter?"

Employee: "Actually not that surprised. Project Y is actually my top priority, and projects like X have taken a full month in the past."

Manager: "So it's unlikely to be done this quarter. When are you 80 percent sure it'll be done by?"

Employee: "I feel 80 percent confident I can deliver it by the end of June."

Manager: "That sounds right. Let me know if that changes."[21]

How would this kind of communication change the way you work?

ARE YOU PREDICTING OR PREACHING?

Before we dive into how to make a good prediction, let's clarify the difference between a *prediction* and a *Prophecy*.

In the previous chapter, we talked about the importance of thinking with both sides of our brain. Remember the windshield wipers, going from left brain to right brain, from data to storytelling, and back again.

Prediction is primarily about the left brain. It's about making hypotheses and being able to measure whether your hypothesis is actually happening. It requires data analytics, logic, and cause-and-effect thinking.

Prophecy is primarily about the right brain. It's about making an empirical judgment and using storytelling to convince others (and yourself). You might even call it preaching.

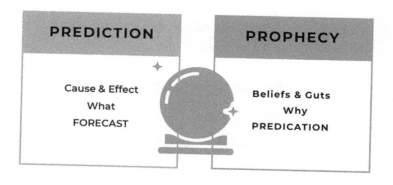

PREDICTION	PROPHECY
Cause & Effect	Beliefs & Guts
What	Why
FORECAST	PREDICATION

If you want to be really good at making Prophecies (not pre-dictions), there is only one rule: make a lot of them. If your Prophecies cover all the potential outcomes, you will always have people who say your "predictions" were right.

In *Superforecasting*, Tetlock makes the distinction between "hedgehogs" and "foxes," based on a 2,500-year-old Greek aph-orism: "The fox knows many things, but the hedgehog knows one big thing."[22]

Tetlock uses the metaphor of the fox to refer to forecasters who often hedge their bets, gather information from as many sources as they can, and change their predictions accordingly. The hedgehogs make their "predictions" (i.e., Prophecies) based on one "Big Idea" and are committed to their conclu-sions regardless of the evidence.[23]

According to Tetlock's research, the foxes consistently out-perform hedgehogs with the accuracy of their predictions. In fact, hedgehogs did a little worse than random guessing—and their accuracy was the *worst* when they were asked about their area of expertise.

"The hedgehog's one Big Idea doesn't improve his foresight. It distorts it," explains Tetlock. "And more information doesn't help because it's all seen through the same tinted glasses. It may increase the hedgehog's confidence, but not his accuracy. That's a bad combination."[24]

We've all seen those experts who go on TV or YouTube and say the same thing over and over again—and end up being wrong, as Tetlock's research reveals. Perhaps they began with prediction, but their ego became so attached to their prediction that it became a Prophecy. And then they repeated their Prophecy publicly for so long that it's not a prediction anymore because they are no longer measuring or correcting their prediction. Now it's a Prophecy.

However, you can start with a Prophecy and end up with a prediction. Most entrepreneurs, when they start up a company, start with the Prophecy, "I believe the market is going to go this direction." For example, when Gabe Newell founded Valve, he believed the future of PC games was free distribution. Was that a gut feeling? Or was it a prediction he could actually back with data?

The truth was the market was just beginning, so it was more of a Prophecy. But he turned his Prophecy into a prediction because he created a specific hypothesis he was able to measure. He tested his hypothesis and measured the company's monthly revenue increase, how many users they had, and how many new games came to market. Then when he talked to investors or employees, he didn't need to preach anymore. (Actually, his business ended up doing so well that he never needed to raise any money from investors.) Now he was making predictions, and he could back up his predictions with measurement and data.

It's not that Prophecy is bad and prediction is good. The best leaders have the ability to shift from left brain to right brain as needed. They can shift from data-driven predictions to story-driven Prophecies. The key is knowing when to use both.

If you don't have any data, the only thing you can do is trust your gut and make a Prophecy. But if you want your organization to be good at making Prophecies and having the same gut instinct, you need to have a very clear value system. Otherwise, you'll just have a lot of individually competing gut instincts.

Imagine a team trying to decide which color to use for the company's branding. Everyone has their own gut instinct, but there's nothing to measure and no common value system. You're left with the strongest ego smashing their fist on the table, saying, "It should be blue, because it has always been blue, and it will always be blue!" competing with the most passionate storyteller, preaching for hours on end about why red is the best choice.

In cases like these, a playbook can provide a clear value system for making good Prophecies. We'll talk more about the playbook in the next chapter.

So when there's nothing to measure, create a Prophecy based on your values and your gut instinct. And then turn your Prophecy into a prediction with the following process, which I will explain in the following sections:

1. Set a hypothesis
2. Measure
3. Change

HOW TO MAKE A PREDICTION
SET A HYPOTHESIS

"The rate of the development of science is not the rate at which you make observations alone but, much more important, the rate at which you create new things to test."

—PHILIP TETLOCK, *SUPERFORECASTING: THE ART AND SCIENCE OF PREDICTION*

If a prediction requires us to measure, then we must begin with something we are able to measure.

That "something" is a hypothesis. A hypothesis is simply a Prophecy you can measure.

The reason why hypotheses are necessary is that humans are extremely bad at predicting what will work. You need to test every idea to overcome this shortcoming.

CASE STUDY: VOODOO

Voodoo, a hyper-casual gaming company based in France, released two games, Numerous Quiz and Fight Light, at the same time.

The team was convinced that Numerous Quiz was a future blockbuster, while Fight Light would fail. Guess what? Numerous Quiz was a miserable failure, and Fight Light, thought to be doomed, was a global hit.

You can never guess what the consumer will like, and you especially cannot assume they will like what you like. You have to test and measure usage and retention KPIs to know if you are going in the right direction.

The key is to create simple hypotheses that cannot only be measured, but measured quickly.

Voodoo has outperformed multibillion-dollar companies because this small company has an incredibly fast iteration cycle. They can go from idea to prototype in a few days: they begin with a fifteen- or twenty-minute conversation, then take about thirty minutes to two hours to draw their prototype and send it to their vendors. Within three days, they will have the pieces they need for AI to begin making video and testing thousands of different combinations of videos, to see if the game has potential or not. They can kill non-winning games very early and then quickly allocate those resources to the winning ideas.

In the end, a hyper-casual game hit is based on two key ingredients: (1) a core gaming mechanic driving usage and retention, and (2) a positive economic equation, where lifetime value is greater than customer acquisition cost (LTV > CAC). (We will focus more on this economic equation in Chapter 4, when we discuss revenue.)

Those two key ingredients are measured, and if a gaming prototype does not pass the cut, it will be abandoned. For instance, Voodoo had three metric thresholds to publish a game: Day 1 retention needed to be greater than 55 percent, Day 7 retention needed to be greater than 22 percent, and cost per install (CPI) needed to be less than $0.25.

There is no space for improvisation. Everything is measured. Both game development and marketing promotion are metric driven.

Their creation process does not stop when the game is published. They keep iterating on the game to increase its lifetime value by refining the design and adding depth to the gameplay.

In 2019, Voodoo was the fourth mobile app publisher by number of downloads—only behind Meta (Facebook, Instagram, WhatsApp), Google (Chrome, Gmail, YouTube), and Bytedance (TikTok)—with more than one billion downloads.

How can a company of 200 to 300 people based in Paris have a bigger mobile phone footprint than Microsoft and Tencent? They have a lightning-fast iteration cycle that begins with simple, testable hypotheses.

If you're having trouble coming up with a hypothesis you can measure, here are some tips:

- Put your hypothesis in a diagram if possible. This exercise simplifies your idea and makes sure you don't have too many things to track.
- To test an ad or an app, pay attention to download time. Most people click away after three seconds if they're not already interested.
- Remember KISS: Keep It Super Simple. Don't overcompli-

cate your hypothesis. The simpler, the better, so you can measure, iterate, and measure again.

MEASURE

"If you can't measure something, don't build it. If you couldn't measure the results, don't try it. Because how do you know it's working? How do you know it isn't?"

—ANDREW TRADER, CO-FOUNDER AND FORMER VP OF
SALES AND BUSINESS DEVELOPMENT, ZYNGA

Once you have your hypothesis, the next step is to measure it.

Zynga became famous as the most data-driven company in the gaming industry because it excelled in what I call the *pendulum framework*.

Since the beginning of humanity, we have used pendulums to know the gender of our baby, to find water, or to otherwise predict the future.

The pendulum framework is a method of predicting the future for your business based on measuring data.

It begins with a set of hypotheses. For example, a set of hypotheses for a gaming company might be the following:

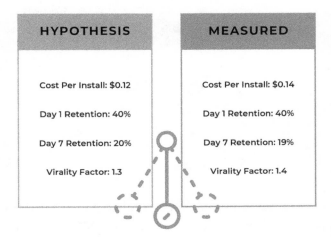

HYPOTHESIS	MEASURED
Cost Per Install: $0.12	Cost Per Install: $0.14
Day 1 Retention: 40%	Day 1 Retention: 40%
Day 7 Retention: 20%	Day 7 Retention: 19%
Virality Factor: 1.3	Virality Factor: 1.4

We expect the virality factor (how many invites sent per player) to be 1.3 percent, we expect day one retention (how many people will come back one day after the install) to be 40 percent, and we expect day seven retention (how many people will come back seven days after they install) to be 20 percent.

In the right column, I will record my measurements.

We create a quick prototype, and indeed, it's very viral; people are sending invites everywhere. We do lots of advertising on Facebook, and we see one day after install that, indeed, 40 percent of the people are coming back. If our hypotheses pretty much equal what we're measuring, the pendulum is right in the center.

If we expected 40 percent day one retention, but we measure 20 percent retention, the pendulum goes to the left. On the other hand, if we expected 40 percent day one retention, and we measure 60 percent, the pendulum goes to the right.

We've hit the results we want for our LTV versus cost of acquisition, and based on what we've measured, we know that if we increase day one retention by 2 percent on a spreadsheet, for example, we'll be able to predict how much it will impact our lifetime value in seven days.

In this way, the pendulum framework provides a system that allows you to make important decisions based on the way the pendulum moves.

If the pendulum is going to the left, that means you've made a wrong assumption. If it's going to the right, either you were very cautious with your prediction, or you're on to something amazing.

CASE STUDY: ZYNGA

Zynga is a social gaming company whose claim to fame is Farm-Ville and also produces games like Zynga Poker and Words with Friends. In May 2022, Take-Two acquired Zynga for $12.7 billion.[25]

One of the most valuable treasures Take-Two acquired was Zynga's access to petabytes of data, which they use to create their products.

Zynga was a pioneer in the area of data analytics and influenced the entire gaming industry to become driven by data rather than pure guts. The company was founded around the same time as Facebook, when game designers primarily made predictions based on gut instinct. In other words, they were making Prophecies, not predictions.

According to founding team member Andrew Trader and founding CEO Mark Pincus, Zynga's core value was its focus on analytics.

Unlike other game studios, Zynga hired product managers with analytics experience from other industries, like finance or consulting, from the start. They were transparent with the data, and everyone had a stake in the metrics—from the CEO on down.[26]

Zynga would decide what metrics to track as they were actually designing the game, based on what actions were involved in the game. Both the metrics and the ability to track the metrics had to be in place prior to launch.

According to previous vice president and general manager Roy Sehgal:

"Our philosophy in the beginning was to fully instrument the product and rigorously test the analytics tracking before launch. We realized the importance of using data to understand user behavior and product performance, and then creatively iterating the product experience post-launch. We would delay a launch if we could not properly track the metrics. Data and analytics were not an afterthought."[27]

Zynga also had a background in social rather than pure game design. What differentiates Zynga from its competitors is the huge volume of user data they have managed to accumulate, which they can use for experimentation and optimization.

Let me explain why this matters so much for a company like Zynga.

In FarmVille, typically less than 2 percent of users will ever make a purchase. In other words, 98 percent of users won't buy anything in the game, even if they play for dozens, hundreds, or even thousands of hours. The people who don't buy anything are monetized through advertising. From time to time, they see an ad, and if they watch a video, they get rewarded with coins, for example, they can use in the game.

It can be very expensive to acquire users. For games like Zynga Poker, acquiring a player can cost between $8 and $50. Yet most of the players won't spend any money and will only be monetized through advertising. So it's very important for Zynga to retain users to generate ad revenue at the very least. It's also important to optimize game mechanics to try to monetize these users as much as they can, once they are retained.

How does a company like Zynga do it? Every user action is

recorded in the system. The product manager will analyze user action and social interaction and from there will guide game improvement. For each iteration of the game, the product manager will collect data, review it, and ultimately create a new feedback loop and hypothesis.

For example, when FarmVille was first created, the animals were purely for decoration. But when Zynga noticed that users seemed to enjoy interacting with the animals, they gave them the opportunity to purchase these virtual animals with real dollars. Then Zynga gave users the opportunity to elevate animals' involvement in FarmVille and create rare animals, which became one of their main sources of revenue.

Buildables are another example, as former Zynga general manager Niko Vuori explains. In games like FarmVille or FrontierVille, players can collect pieces to create a buildable, like a house or a car. They can either collect these pieces from Facebook friends or buy the pieces as an in-game purchase.

Studying the data, Zynga realized that players were not motivated to purchase pieces for buildables until they were almost finished assembling them. They would collect the first few pieces from friends, but they generally wouldn't purchase pieces until they got closer to the end. The closer they got to finishing the buildable, the more willing they were to pay for the last piece or two. They wouldn't pay for progress, but they would pay for completion.

Zynga monetized this user behavior by making buildables that were easy to start with items they could collect from their network of friends, but hard to complete without making a purchase.[28]

Zynga's co-founder Andrew Trader became famous for saying, "If you cannot measure something, don't do it." Remember, Zynga was founded at a time when almost no company was measuring anything—including gaming companies. People came up with a good idea, or a customer would suggest an idea, and they would just do it. But they would not measure anything. Zynga's founding team focused on making better predictions, which not only made them incredibly successful, but revolutionized the entire industry.

CHANGE

After you measure, you make whatever improvements are needed based on the data you collected, create a new hypothesis, and start the prediction cycle over again.

According to Gabe Newell of Valve, "The most important thing you can do is to get into an iteration cycle where you can measure the impact of your work, have a hypothesis about how making changes will affect those variables, and ship changes regularly. It doesn't even matter that much what the content is—it's the iteration of hypothesis, changes, and measurement that will make you better at a faster rate than anything else we have seen."[29]

Once you reach a product/market fit and your customer lifetime value exceeds your acquisition costs, you scale.

"To be perfect is to change often."

—WINSTON CHURCHILL

In fact, there is ultimately one thing that matters for investors, which is what should also matter to the entrepreneur: do you have a user acquisition channel that can scale? Can you reliably put in $100 and get $120? Can you put in $1 million and get $1.2 million?

In my case, for example, I'm an investor in an algorithmic trading company, where bots buy and sell things almost instantaneously. Six transactions can take place within twenty milliseconds. In our pendulum framework, we have a dashboard where on one side, we have the bots' predictions that if we buy this at this price and resell at that price, we will make X percent profit and can allocate X dollars to it. On the other side, we have the measurements of what the bot actually did, which are nearly identical to its predictions. Where the bot predicts we should buy at $100, it buys at $100. Where the bot predicts we should sell at $101 to make 1 percent profit, it sells at $101.1, and we make 1.1 percent profit. All of this happens within milliseconds—and we don't lose.

It takes a bit of mathematics and a bit of investment strategy, but it's not very complicated. With the code, you don't need a team of twenty people; you need only a handful. And every day you're earning.

The most scalable industry is finance, because it's purely digits on the internet. You don't need to produce anything. But if you have a good product, with good prediction skills, anything can scale like this.

Hypothesize, measure, change, repeat. How fast you cycle through these steps is how fast you can scale.

As Peter Drucker said long ago, "The best way to predict the future is to invent it."

GAME ON: PREDICTION

☐ **Bring the power of prediction to the people.** How might you begin shifting more of your decisions to your team?

☐ **Learn how to predict.** Are you teaching your team how to predict and use mathematical probabilities in their daily work? Are you focusing on the process rather than results?

☐ **Know the difference between prediction and Prophecy.** Do you know the difference between prediction and Prophecy—and when to do both?

☐ **Practice the prediction cycle of hypothesis, measure, change, and repeat.** In what area of your business can you begin practicing the prediction cycle of set a hypothesis, measure, change, repeat?

Chapter 3

PLAYBOOK

"There is no favorable wind for the sailor who doesn't know where to go."

—SENECA

One day, not long ago, I went to the playground with my then ten-year-old daughter, Miya. She was soon joined by five or so of her friends, and I suggested, "Hey, why don't you go and play something together?"

I threw them a ball, and instantly they began running in every direction. One took the ball with his hands and threw it, while another kid kicked it as hard as she could. Yet another one grabbed the ball and began chasing the others, trying to throw it at them to tag them. Soon they were exhausted, and when one accidentally got hit in the face—it was game over. As I walked over, surveying the damage, I decided to use another strategy.

"Hey guys," I said. "Why don't we play soccer instead?" I quickly reviewed the rules with them, although most knew them already.

I created two teams, and since one team was one player short, I joined that team as goalie.

We ended up playing for two hours. It was a lot of fun, and there were no injuries.

What I had realized earlier, after one of the kids got smashed in the head, was that they were playing an infinite game. In gaming, infinite games are games with no common rules, so the game literally changes every time new players join.

Humans are designed for finite games, not infinite games. In fact, that's what game companies do: they design rules and turn infinite games into finite games.

As a player, the first thing a gamer does before playing the game is understand the rules of the game so they know how to win. If it's a team game, each teammate plays a specific role in winning the game.

For example, soccer is played according to a set of rules. You use a single round ball called the soccer ball (or football), and there are two teams with usually eleven players each (although in our case, we were playing three on three). Each team competes to get the ball into the other team's goal, and that's how you score a goal. The team with the most goals at the end of the game wins. That's the kind of game humans are good at.

Now think of your business. Are you playing a finite game or an infinite game? Do you know exactly what it takes to win at your business? If you're playing with a team, do you and your team members know what role you play in winning? When you or your team members wake up in the morning, do you know exactly what you're going to do that day to win at your role?

If you are exhausted when you go to bed at night but feel like you are achieving nothing, you may be playing an infinite game. You may be confused about the rules, or simply overwhelmed by playing too many roles at once. Maybe your team members feel the same way.

Another sign that you may be playing an infinite game is if you have a lot of "traffic control" meetings. A traffic control meeting is typically when a team member comes to you with an idea and asks for approval. Then you go to the manager, who plays the role of the traffic light: yes is green, maybe is amber, and red is no.

If you're having a lot of traffic control meetings, it could be because your people don't fully understand the rules of the game, or even know which game they're playing—so they don't know what strategy to use to win as a team.

FOCUSING EQUALS WINNING

Many businesses end up playing an infinite game because (1) they don't set the rules of the game, and as a result, (2) they try to be all things to all people all the time. Sport, in contrast, is a very clear example of a finite game, which is why you end up with 2.3 billion soccer fans, for example.

Tom Brady, one of the most awarded players in the history of the NFL, said, "Winners focus on winning; losers focus on winners." If you want to change your business from an infinite game to a finite game, the real answer comes from Tom Brady: focus on winning, and stop focusing on others.

"Winners focus on winning; losers focus on winners."

—TOM BRADY

Are you constantly reacting to what your customers or your people are asking for, trying to be all things to all people—or are you following the rules of your business's game? Are you focused on what your competitors are doing and constantly reacting to their new offers, or are you focused on winning at your business's game? Don't be led by the fear of losing, but instead focus on executing and winning.

When it comes to focus, the first thing you must do is to learn to say no. Saying no might irritate other people, maybe even those on your team, but Steve Jobs, founder of Apple, said that innovation means saying no to a thousand things. Focusing is about saying no, not yes. He also famously said, "I'm actually as proud of the things we haven't done as the things we have done."[30]

Similarly, investor Warren Buffett has said, "The difference between successful people and really successful people is that really successful people say no to almost everything."[31] This can be a challenging lesson for those who believe success means saying yes to every opportunity. If that's you, perhaps you should be practicing your "no" responses and using them more often!

If you feel exhausted but aren't sure what you're getting done each day, if you're having a lot of traffic control meetings, or if you're constantly reacting to others' demands, then you might need a *playbook*. A playbook tells you what game you're playing, the rules of the game, and how to win together.

As a gamer, I see life as a series of games. Sometimes you lose, sometimes you win, and most of us like winning more than we like losing. Those who say they don't mind losing, or that just playing the game is the most important thing, are probably a little checked out. Maybe life has been hard, maybe they've gotten used to losing, and that's okay.

The most important question for business leaders is, Are you playing to win, or are you playing not to lose? In gaming, we call it *least mode* versus *beast mode*. Least mode is when you're playing not to lose. People in least mode tend to be either reactive or a little checked out, both out of fear of losing. As long as they're not losing, they're typically putting forth minimal effort.

In contrast, if you're in beast mode, you're playing to win. You're a lot more proactive and focused on achievement. Your energy is volcanic and infectious; you're doing whatever is necessary to move forward. Usually you possess absolute conviction that you will win. From a chemical point of view, your brain is creating oxytocin and dopamine, the feel-good chemicals you need to win. (That's why game designers work on orchestrating oxytocin and dopamine hits on a daily basis when they make games.)

LEAST MODE	BEAST MODE
PLAYING NOT TO LOSE	PLAYING TO WIN
Playing Defense	Playing Offense
Do the minimal effort to avoid losing	Do whatever it takes to win
Disbelief	Conviction
Reactive/Passive	Proactive
Prevention Focus	Achievement Focus

If you're in a play-to-win mode, you have no doubts and you have no fear. You focus on making the most of your strengths. You don't make excuses for anything, and you take calculated risks; you're typically resourceful. Playing to win is a self-fulfilling prophecy: the more you fixate on the positive outcome, the more likely it is to come to fruition.

Think about your team members and maybe even yourself: who is playing to win, and who is playing not to lose?

To play to win, you have to know the rules of the game.

In this chapter, we're going to cover how to create the kind of playbooks gaming companies use, so you cannot only have a lot more fun in your business, but you can shift your entire team from least mode to beast mode and play to win.

THE MUM MODEL

When it comes to standard operating procedures, one of the major differences between a traditional company and a tech or gaming company is that a traditional company typically starts with "what," or the result, while a tech or gaming company, in the words of author Simon Sinek, starts with "why." They focus more on their values, their mission, who they want to serve, and how they're going to serve them rather than the result.

Unlike traditional companies that tell people what to do, tech and gaming companies tell them why. If we know exactly what to do, we try to automate those tasks as much as possible with codes and AI, which usually cost nearly nothing to operate, once built. But if the "what" requires thought, this is where people come into play. (It sounds simple, but as we've seen with the reverse pyramid model, it's not as easy as it sounds.)

The playbook framework I'm going to introduce to you also starts with why. It's called the MUM model, because just as a mum cares the most for her child, this playbook will allow you to care most for your business, your team, your customers, and even yourself.

MUM stands for the following:

- Mission: Why are we here? What do we value?
- User: Who do we serve?
- Method: How do we make decisions, prioritize, and allocate resources to fulfill our mission and serve our users?

The purpose of the MUM model is both to instill clarity and to create a culture of empowerment *and* performance. When you start with why and your people know how to win at their jobs, they can be focused on action rather than playing politics or trying to game the system.

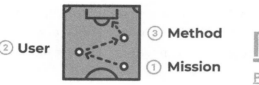

MISSION: WHAT'S YOUR MOONSHOT?

"Cherish your vision and your dreams as they are the children of your soul, the blueprints of your ultimate achievements."

—NAPOLEON HILL

Your playbook begins with your *mission*—and not just any mission, but a bold mission. The tech and gaming industries typically aim for a bold vision and make it bigger.

Many traditional businesses consider making a profit their primary mission (whether they say it directly or not). Ironically, focusing on profit alone as a mission may keep you from achieving it.

Consider Justine Musk's answer to this question on Quora: "Will I become a billionaire if I am determined to be one and put in all the necessary work required?" (Justine Musk is Elon Musk's ex-wife.)

No.

One of the many qualities that separate self-made billionaires from the rest of us is their ability to ask the right questions. This is not the right question. (Which is not to say it's a bad question. It just won't get that deep part of your mind working to help you—mulling things over when you think you're thinking about something else—sending up flares of insight.)

You're determined. So what? You haven't been racing naked through shark-infested waters yet. Will you be just as determined when you wash up on some deserted island, disoriented and bloody and ragged and beaten and staring into the horizon with no sign of rescue?

We live in a culture that celebrates determination and hard work, but understand: these are the qualities that keep you in the game after most everybody else has left, or until somebody bigger and stronger picks you up and hurls you back out to sea. Determination and hard work are necessary, yes, but they are the minimum requirements. As in: the bare minimum.

A lot of people work extremely hard and through no fault of their own—bad luck, the wrong environment, unfortunate circumstances—struggle to survive. How can you *leverage* your time and your work?

Shift your focus away from what you want (a billion dollars) and get deeply, intensely curious about what the world wants and needs.

Ask yourself what you have the potential to offer that is so unique and compelling and helpful that no computer could replace you, no one could outsource you, no one could steal your product and make it better and then club you into oblivion (not literally).

Then develop that potential. Choose one thing and become a master of it.

Choose a second thing and become a master of that.

When you become a master of two worlds (say, engineering and business), you can bring them together in a way that will a) introduce hot ideas to each other, so they can have idea sex and make idea babies that no one has seen before and b) create a competitive advantage because you can move between worlds, speak both languages, connect the tribes, mash the elements to spark fresh creative insight until you wake up with the epiphany that changes your life.

The world doesn't throw a billion dollars at a person because the person wants it or works so hard they feel they deserve it. (The world does not care what you want or deserve.)

The world gives you money in exchange for something it perceives to be of equal or greater value: something that transforms an aspect of the culture, reworks a familiar story or introduces a new one, alters the way people think about the category and make use of it in daily life.

There is no roadmap, no blueprint for this; a lot of people will give you a lot of advice, and most of it will be bad, and a lot of it will be good and sound but you'll have to figure out how it doesn't apply to you because you're coming from an unexpected angle.

And you'll be doing it alone, until you develop the charisma and credibility to attract the talent you need to come with you.

Have courage. (You will need it.)

And good luck. (You'll need that too.)[32]

Your mission is the most important thing to internalize and then communicate to your team, because a strong mission is what flips the switch from least mode to beast mode. A mission of producing profit is not strong enough to flip the switch. For that, you need a transformational mission.

MOONSHOT THINKING

Think of your transformational mission as a *moonshot*. In 1962, United States president John F. Kennedy spoke at Rice University and said, "We choose to go to the moon in this decade." A moonshot is a concrete goal that may seem impossible, and you only discover it is possible after it is achieved. JFK did not set that goal knowing how to achieve it or believing it would be easy. He simply aligned an entire country to a bold vision with a specific time frame and inspired his country to take action.

Not very long after John F. Kennedy's speech at Rice, in 1978, Deng Xiaoping was launching another moonshot in China. He quoted an old proverb: "It doesn't matter if the cat is black or white, so long as it catches mice."[33] With these words, Deng also aligned an entire country to a bold vision: to combine socialism with free enterprise and emerge out of poverty. Deng did not set that goal knowing how to achieve it or promising it would be easy. He simply set out to accomplish something incredible, with technology being one of China's fundamental pillars of social and economic transformation.

Deng Xiaoping became known as the "Architect of Modern China," putting China on track to become one of the fastest-growing economies in the world. Deng's socialism with Chinese characteristics raised the standard of living of hundreds of millions.[34]

Following JFK and Deng's examples of moonshot thinking, large technology companies such as Tencent and Google are building "moonshot factories."

As a moonshot factory, Google X (known as X) is a place where "the processes and culture make it easier to make radical breakthroughs—repeatedly."

X's essential ingredients for a moonshot include the following:

1. A huge problem in the world that affects millions or billions of people
2. A radical, sci-fi-sounding solution that may seem impossible today
3. A technology breakthrough that gives us a glimmer of hope that the solution could be possible in the next five to ten years[35]

Moonshot *thinking* is when you choose a massive problem, such as climate change, and then propose a radical solution to the problem using a disruptive technology and associated business model.

Taken a step further, following the model of the gaming industry, moonshot thinking:

1. Combines breakthrough technologies, such as artificial intelligence, with disruptive business practices and models
2. Distributes and prices items differently
3. Develops communities

This kind of bold mission, or moonshot, is what will not only allow your business to become one of the most profitable in your industry, but it will shift your entire team from least mode to beast mode.

How might you apply moonshot thinking in your industry? Could your business be a moonshot factory?

10X IS EASIER THAN 10 PERCENT

With moonshot thinking, forget the idea of 10 percent incremental improvement. Instead, focus on a solution that brings ten times (10x) improvement or completely solves it.

"Here is the surprising truth," says Astro Teller, CEO of X—Alphabet's moonshot factory. "It's often *easier* to make something ten times better than it is to make it ten percent better."

Why? Because, as Teller explains, when you focus on making something 10 percent better, you're still using the same tools, the same design assumptions, and the same kind of thinking. Although we may think we're doing the right thing by working hard and persevering when we don't see much progress, the truth is we may *never* see progress with this set of assumptions. When you focus on making something 10x better, you change your assumptions and your thinking entirely.[36]

And here is the surprising truth that game serial killers like Supercell or Voodoo know: it is often easier to make something ten times better *from scratch* than trying to make something that already exists 10 percent better.

The core metrics observed in the early days of a game are usually the metrics you carry for years. If a game does not have the right metrics built into its DNA from the start, it is often more productive to start a new game idea from scratch than to iterate again and again.

As Teller says, "Kennedy understood that the size of the challenge actually motivates people: that bigger challenges create passion... That's what 10x does that 10 percent could never do. 10x can light a fire in hearts."[37]

As the leader of your company, train yourself and your team to be moonshot thinkers. What matters most to you? What is your 10x moonshot? Let that be your mission, and see how it ignites your team to do the impossible.

But as you pursue your moonshot, don't be surprised when you encounter risk and failure along the way.

A few years ago, Jeff Weiner, then-CEO of LinkedIn, came to China to discuss the possibility of LinkedIn entering China. A breakfast meeting was planned with about fifteen people, including myself. To prepare for this meeting, I had asked a few of my Chinese entrepreneur friends what they thought. Based on their responses, I had prepared an answer that said, in short, "You can try, but you're just going to waste your time, and it's not going to go anywhere." And I had my reasons ready to explain.

When it was my turn, I stepped up and did my best to explain to one of the most respected and admired CEOs from one of the biggest Silicon Valley companies why he was going to lose in China. He listened carefully, and then responded, "I'm going to explain to you why I believe you're right, and yet I'm still going to launch in China."

Here is my summary of his answer: He said LinkedIn's mission is to connect the world for professionals, and China includes one-third of professionals worldwide. "We cannot fulfill our mission if we ignore one-third of the world's professionals who are in China," he said. "So even if we don't make a lot of money, and even if it takes years, we have to do it because this is our mission. We cannot ignore one-third of the world."

Indeed, LinkedIn entered the Chinese market, a venture that was largely funded by the VC firm Sequoia China, and it was a failure from a product adoption point of view. However, when Microsoft acquired LinkedIn for $25 billion, it was rumored that LinkedIn China, the "failed" business product, was valued at one billion dollars as part of the deal—which was both a success for LinkedIn, its investors, including Sequoia, and the local team running LinkedIn China who had stock options.

What is your moonshot? What ignites such passion in you and

your team that it would be worth trying and failing at? That is your mission.

After identifying their moonshot, many organizations find it helpful to create a roadmap to achieve that moonshot, breaking down their mission into five-year, one-year, and thirty-day plans.

Your five-year plan is your long-term vision. What will your company be known for? What customers will you serve? What kind of team will you have?

From there, think of the three things your organization needs to be great at to achieve its five-year vision. This is your one-year plan.

Then, for your thirty-day plan, think of what things you will need to work on in the next thirty days to move toward that one-year vision.

Moonshot Thinking		5-YEARS 1-YEAR 30-DAYS

Another way to create a roadmap is the well-known *Merlin Exercise*, used by organizational process consultant Martin Ramsay and many others.[38] As Ramsay explains, in T. H. White's book *The Once and Future King*, the magician Merlin lived backwards through time, such that he "remembered the future" but could not remember the past—because for him, the past hadn't happened yet. But this ability to remember the future was very useful to King Arthur!

The Merlin Exercise is about "remembering the future" of your organization and creating a roadmap for your moonshot.

1. Imagine you have successfully achieved your moonshot. Where are you? Who are you with? What are you doing? What are you *not* doing?
2. Next, imagine you are halfway to your moonshot. What is happening? What tasks have you completed? What tasks are left to achieve?
3. Then imagine what it will be like if you are a quarter of the way there, asking yourself the same questions.
4. Continue taking one step closer to the present until your next actions are clear. These actions are the beginning of your roadmap.

CASE STUDY: ROVIO

Peter Vesterbacka, also known as Mighty Eagle, is co-founder of the Finnish company Rovio, the maker of Angry Birds.

Peter is a living legend in the Finnish mobile gaming industry. He is probably one of the most well-known characters in the gaming industry worldwide and widely acknowledged as the father of the Nordic startup revolution. In addition to cofounding Rovio, Peter has also worked at Hewlett-Packard, and founded Slush, the biggest tech conference in the Nordics, and Mobile Monday, among others. In 2011, *TIME* magazine put Peter on their list of the world's hundred most influential people.

After Rovio's successful one billion-dollar IPO in 2014, Peter decided to leave Rovio Entertainment in 2016. He has since been an investor and advisor to growing companies. He is also digging a 15-billion-dollar underwater tunnel. This tunnel aims to link Finland with Estonia, making it the longest underwater tunnel in history, longer than the France-UK Eurotunnel.

How do you go from racking up billions of downloads with a hit game featuring birds, to building the world's longest undersea tunnel?

If you get to know Peter, and I have known Peter for over a dozen years now, this is not as surprising as it first seems. Born and raised in Western Finland, in the beautiful coastal city of Pori, his philosophy is to aim big, keep going, and learn along the way.

In his trademark uniform, a red hoodie, jeans, and red sneakers, Peter always enthusiastically shares his valuable entrepreneurial experience.

Peter noted that Rovio created 51 games before making Angry Birds. No one remembers any of the games before Angry Birds, the Finnish firm's 52nd attempt to make a mobile hit game. Angry Birds has gotten over 5 billion downloads since the series' launch in 2009. That equals 65 percent of the world's population (7.8 billion), for comparison's sake. There were more downloads of the game than there are people in Africa, Oceania, and Europe combined. Nine out of ten people in both China and the US know the brand.

"I thought I was super-ambitious in 2010 when I said we'll make one hundred million dollars and everyone else thought I was crazy, but it's very important people thought I was insane for saying one hundred million back then," said Peter.[39]

In February 2011, Angry Birds became the fastest growing game in history, with five hundred million downloads in less than two years. Angry Birds was then the number one game in 79 countries, with 266 billion levels and 400 billion birds shot. Gamers worldwide played the game for 300 million minutes daily, which adds up to 570 years daily.[40]

"This is very important though: we hope we know what we are doing, but we do not always," said Peter to *The Guardian* in 2012. "We're learning every day, and getting better in the toy business, the book business, the games business... It's okay to make mistakes, especially if you're going into new areas and doing things differently."[41]

In 2013, hundreds of millions of people played Angry Birds each month, which according to Peter was the size of their Twitter following.[42] Angry Birds then reached one billion downloads, the first-ever Finnish game company to hit such a mark, setting a new target for other companies in Finland. Since then, two others hit that target—Fingersoft with Hill Climbing Racing, and Supercell with Clash of Clans. Others in neighboring countries like Sweden have since surpassed that mark with Candy Crush by King (now a part of Activision) currently holding the crown of 2.7 billion downloads. And Mojang (now part of Microsoft) has Minecraft.

In January 2014, Angry Birds reached the 2 billion mark, the same time Rovio's IPO was valued at a billion dollars. At that point, Rovio went beyond gaming, launching mostly self-funded movies that generated $350 million each at the box office.

By July 2015, Angry Birds downloads added up to more than

three billion collectively. Nearly 5 billion downloads across all platforms have been counted to date.

Angry Birds grew so fast because Rovio was well positioned with the right product at the right time, early in the launch of a new platform, the Apple iPhone.

"We're not building Angry Birds for a hundred days but for a hundred years," Peter said. "Mario is a great role model for anyone in games; it's been built for almost thirty years now. Hello Kitty is forty this year [in 2014], and Mickey Mouse was launched in 1928 as a black-and-white cartoon, and that company is now building theme parks based on the character on every continent."[43] Rovio was aiming to "create a long-lasting, global brand" with Angry Birds.[44]

"The reason we grew that big was because we kept aiming higher. We were not building Angry Birds for a hundred days, but for a hundred years."

—PETER VESTERBACKA, CO-FOUNDER OF ROVIO

And the company went way beyond making games. They expanded into merchandising with characters: Angry Birds Toons, a TV series, and two Angry Birds Movies. There are also Angry Birds theme parks on every continent, Angry Birds drinks, and Angry Birds Playground books. Partnerships included NASA, Star Wars, Puzzle & Dragon (the top-grossing game in Japan), singers like Shakira, and a geolocalization game with McDonald's a few years before Pokemon Go.

Peter probably benefited from his previous life in marketing at HP, where he started working at age twenty-four and then led a global innovation and corporate partnership program. He believes in doing things differently.

"We don't spend any money on traditional advertising. We're all about doing special events, like launching *Angry Birds Space* in space with NASA. No other game has been launched in space. We thought, "why not?"... We're a tiny company of 300 from a tiny country. By necessity, we have to do things differently and smarter. In the end, marketing is not about the money."[45]

Spending enough time in the region, you learn and appreciate a well-known Finnish term "sisu." It roughly translates as toughness and perseverance, critical elements of the Finnish character. This toughness and perseverance are required for all startups, each with their challenges and obstacles, to progress.

Now Peter's moonshot is to build a tunnel between Helsinki, the capital city of Finland, and Tallinn, Estonia's capital. The proposed tunnel starts from the Tallinn airport, dips in the Baltic Sea, and has an artificial island in the middle.

"Building a tunnel is different from building a game, but not that different," Peter said. "It is about making things happen. Bringing the right people together." And when people were skeptical about his ability to execute on his vision, he answered, "If they choose to underestimate my ability to make stuff happen, it is their problem."[46]

Finnish people often joke that they can walk on water. It may seem impossible, but the Finns take it in stride when the winter reaches its coldest and snowiest time. They make the most out of it by using the frozen ocean as a winter playground. It is not difficult anymore to start a business once you have found the right way to bring your ideas to fruition.

PETER VESTERBACKA'S MOONSHOT TIPS

- Aim big, keep going, and learn along the way.
- Try to know what you're doing, but it's okay if you don't always. It's okay to make mistakes, especially if you're going into new areas and doing things differently.
- It is very important that people think you are insane for aiming high. Let them think it is crazy talk, then reach it and prove them wrong.
- Don't create a product for one hundred days; instead, create a long-lasting, global brand.
- Keep going, the *sisu* way.

USERS: WHO DO YOU WANT TO SERVE?

When considering whether to invest in a company, I usually look very carefully at the connection the founders have with the community they want to serve.

Listening to a bunch of executives describe customer challenges, define prospect and buyer profiles, and explain how to manage potential objections might have worked at some point, but not anymore.

Competition is ferocious. A team who deeply connects with the users they serve and their problems will outperform their competition every time.

Why? There are many ways to answer this question, but it can be summed up in something Zig Ziglar once said:

"You will get all you want in life if you help enough other people get what they want."

Here is how ClickFunnels founder Russell Brunson puts it (you will read more about his story in Chapter 5):

When I look at all these amazing people changing the lives of tens of thousands (and in some cases millions) of people, almost all of them have felt an internal pull to want to serve and help people. It's almost like a voice inside them telling them they are destined for greatness. Yet at the same time, they have this other voice that consistently tells them they're inadequate, that they're not enough. Not smart enough, not focused enough, not thin enough, not experienced enough, not good enough...

The strange thing is that often the more they do and the more people they help, the louder the voice of inadequacy becomes. Whether you're just starting this journey or you've been at it for a while, just know that the biggest hurdle you're likely to face is being okay with positioning yourself as an expert. What's equally important to understand is you're not alone. I really feel for people struggling with that negative inner voice because, in all honesty, that's the way I often feel.

I feel like I have been blessed beyond what any human being should ever be blessed with on this Earth. And I feel that this gift I've been given from God is something I must share. In fact, if I don't share it, that would be an injustice to Him and the people I could serve. Yet as I am out there in the trenches every single day building companies, working with entrepreneurs, trying to change the world in my own little way, I still wrestle with these feelings of inadequacy.

As I talk to people, I realize that these same feelings keep most people from ever taking on the mantle of an expert. The voice keeps them from stepping up and stepping into that role. And it's a tragedy for a couple of reasons. First, it deprives them of the experience and the opportunities they should have. And more importantly, it deprives the people whose lives they could change. Those people you could serve by sharing your God-given talents and expert abilities—they might never be reached.

So I want to pause here and take a moment, not so much to convince you that you're an expert, but to give you whatever permission you might need to be able to move forward. You have the ability—and, I believe, the responsibility—to serve others with your gifts, whatever they are. You've been blessed with talents, ideas, and unique abilities that have gotten you to where you are in life, and those gifts were given to you so you could share them with others. There are people today who need what you have. And they are just waiting for you to find your voice, so you can help them change their lives. What a tragedy for them if you don't develop your voice now...

For every political, social, or religious movement throughout history, the charismatic leader paints a picture of the future they are trying to create and what life will be like when they get there... For you to have success in this business, you have to give your followers hope of something better so they will be perceptive to the change you are going to offer them. You do that by painting a vision of the future that they want. Most people want to cast all their faith and personal responsibility into something bigger than themselves. It happens in religion, it happens in political movements, it happens in the workplace, and it will be true for your movement as well. People want to plug into something bigger than themselves, so it's your job to create that vision.

If you're going to start a mass movement and create a vehicle for change, the first question you have to ask yourself is "WHO do I want to serve?" The answer to that question is typically people who were just like you before you became an expert, right? As a charismatic leader, you're going to lead people on a path you've walked before.[47]

Do you too have that internal pull to serve others? If so, you too are destined for greatness.

So if you have a bold mission and you want to start a mass movement, the next question is "Who do I want to serve?"

Who are your users?

Your "users" are the ones you are responsible for serving. They are the people you relate to and care for. You might even become a charismatic leader for them, because you listen to them, you feel them, and they relate to you.

"You will get all you want in life if you help enough other people get what they want."

—ZIG ZIGLAR

Once you've identified who you want to serve, you'll need to dig a few layers deeper to find your specific audience.

Should you serve a big total addressable market?

Should you have access to the users already?

Should you be able to relate to these users?

Or should you simply *want* to serve these users?

Ideally, all of the above.

To define your ideal audience, you can use the BRAW framework, where BRAW stands for

- a *big* addressable market
- whom you can *relate* to,
- have *access* to,
- and *want* to serve.

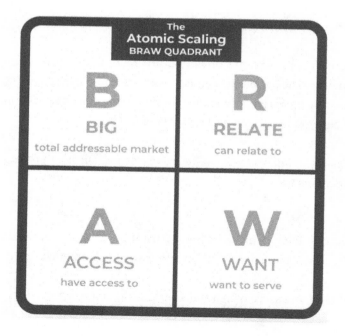

By the way, if you're not familiar with the Scottish word *braw*, it means excellent or pleasant. If you say, "Oh, he's such a braw lad," that means he's a very pleasant guy to be around, very handsome and smart, a brave mate.

Which "BRAW users" do you want to serve?

CASE STUDY: DISCORD

Discord, which currently has over one hundred million daily active users, was originally a game company founded by Jason Citron. Jason was a League of Legends player, which at the time was one of the most popular games on PC, and he was trying to figure out how to make a game like League of Legends on mobile.

At the same time, as a League of Legends player, he got to know a lot of players on the PC game and collected a lot of feedback. Ultimately, they identified that the big problem for League of Legends players was voice communication. It wasn't easy to do voice communication within League of Legends itself, and although most people used Skype as a solution, at that time the quality was not very good.

As a side project, one of the lead engineers at Discord thought, *Hey, let's just develop an open source voice application, just to make it easier for League of Legends players to play together. And maybe we can use this voice application as a way to recruit League of Legends players and hopefully to get them to play our mobile game.*

That's exactly what happened. They developed a product to acquire users on the cheap by providing them with a solution to a significant problem. At that point, they decided to pivot from making games to focusing solely on the voice application (which I find really interesting from a business point of view).

Here's another interesting fact: They decided to make this pivot literally days after Tencent invested a few million dollars in their company to make games. As you can probably guess, Tencent is a highly desirable investor. Yet they essentially told Tencent, "Oh, by the way—we realize we've been pitching you for the last six months about this awesome game we're going to make, and you just invested a few million dollars in our company, but sorry, we're not going to make games anymore. If you want, we can give you your money back." Fortunately, Tencent said, "No, it's fine; you guys do whatever you feel is right."

Nearly overnight, Discord was worth over 5 billion dollars.

How did Jason and his team know this was the right thing to do? And how did Tencent know this was a good investment?

They followed the BRAW framework:

They had a big total addressable market. The League of Legends players alone were enough of a market for them to develop something really big.

They could relate to the users. They were themselves League of Legends players, and they all had the same problem.

They had access to their users. Because they were players, they ended up befriending a lot of the top players on the internet.

They wanted to serve them. That was pretty clear, as one of their team members developed this voice app as a side project.

"People don't care how much you know until they know how much you care."

—THEODORE ROOSEVELT

CASE STUDY: RAZER

Razer has extraordinary clarity about who they are serving. It's right in their tagline: "By Gamers, For Gamers."

Min-Liang Tan, the founder of Razer, doesn't fit the typical profile of a gamer. He is a trained lawyer originally from Singapore, yet he defines himself not as a lawyer—he quit doing that a long time ago—but as a gamer. And as a gamer, if he wants something, he develops it.

For instance, he recently had a back issue and ended up designing a chair for gamers, which is now probably one of the best chairs on the market. He travels a lot, so he designed a laptop for gamers. He plays a lot of games on his phone, so he designed a phone for gamers.

Razer had the biggest IPO in Hong Kong in 2020, which helped make Min one of the richest people in Singapore, as well as one of its youngest billionaires.

Many non-gamers end up using Razer's products for all kinds of reasons because they are incredible products. But Min doesn't care. He's here to serve gamers, and gamers are served.

METHOD: HOW WILL YOU SERVE YOUR USERS?

Once you have a bold mission and your BRAW users, what *method* will you use to serve your users? Your method is your strategy for fulfilling your mission for your users.

Ultimately, I believe every entrepreneur should have the same method, which is the Atomic Scaling method of 3P3R.

How can companies with different missions and different users all have the same method?

It comes back to what we learned in the Prediction chapter.

Prediction is as important as production. Most entrepreneurs tend to focus on a product or service as the method, often without knowing if their customers even want it. If we want an Atomic Scaling company, instead of focusing on building the perfect product or service, we should focus on building a machine to serve our BRAW users with the products and services they want, which at the same time allows us to fulfill our mission.

We're going to talk in detail about how to do this in Part Two, but here is a simple example that illustrates the mindset shift that's needed.

The idea is to begin not with building a product, but with building a sales funnel, where the product is just one part.

As Jack Welch said, "Strategy is simply resource allocation." Here we can simply substitute the word *method* for *strategy*: method is simply resource allocation.

"Strategy is simply resource allocation."

—JACK WELCH

For example, let's say an entrepreneur has a certain budget to invest in starting a new company. The typical entrepreneur would allocate all their resources to building the product, and then pray that someone will buy it. Then, when they inevitably run out of cash, they may ask their friends or family for more cash, or they may simply assume their product was a bad idea, give up on their company, and go back to whatever they were doing before.

But they haven't even given themselves a chance. They never went through the prediction cycle of hypothesis, measurement, and change.

To illustrate a better method, let's play a game. Let's say you are an entrepreneur who has $10,000 to allocate to your new company. In this game, you're going to split your $10,000 into three budgets: $1,000, $2,000, and $7,000. For each budget, you will put 50 percent into prediction and 50 percent into sales. In this case, prediction includes creating a hypothesis about your product or service, testing it, and improving it, and sales includes tasks like buying ads and creating a website. This will force you to properly allocate your resources in a way that will allow you to scale.

Think of the first budget as stage one, where you have $1,000 to show that this idea is going somewhere. If you put 50 percent into prediction and 50 percent into sales, that means you have $500 to build the product (your hypothesis) and $500 to sell it. Even in stage one, you have enough to buy some Facebook ads and set up a simple website. After that, you will collect feedback (measure) and also ask questions like, "Am I still excited about my product? Does it still make sense? How am I going to sell it?" Based on your answers to these questions, you will decide how to improve it (change) and move on to stage two.

Congratulations! In stage two, your budget is $2,000. Here $1,000 will go to prediction, where you will improve your product based on your data from stage one, and $1,000 will go to sales. Then you test it and measure again: "How is my product now? And how are my sales?" You decide what changes to make based on what you measure, and then you move to stage three.

Finally, in stage three, you have $7,000: $3,500 for prediction and $3,500 for sales. How is your product now? How is your sales process? What will you improve?

The idea is to iterate as quickly as you can to get data on what to change *and* on what's working. You're able to quickly change what's not working and get sales more quickly for what is working.

The prediction cycle helps improve products that aren't yet what your users want, and it also forces shy entrepreneurs to share their value with more people, so you can scale faster.

CASE STUDY: ATOMIC SCALING BOOTCAMP FOR KIDS

During the pandemic, I ran a ten-day business bootcamp for the kids in my community. They ranged in age from eleven to seventeen, and were mostly girls—probably because I have daughters and many of them were my daughters' friends.

At the beginning of the bootcamp, none of them knew what kind of business they wanted to start. But after ten days, they all had a business, meaning they had a product and the ability to sell online. Most created a business to support a cause, and some of the kids are still selling today. The one who has done the best is a twelve-year-old whose profits go to an autism association.

Even today, many girls grow up believing they must marry a successful man to be successful themselves. One of my objectives in teaching Atomic Scaling to kids and teenagers, especially girls, is to make sure girls know they don't need to rely on boys. They can do whatever they want in life, because they are already providing for themselves.

The pro level of prediction is *automation*, which is the future for nearly every industry. For example, shoe companies can produce prototypes through 3D printing and only produce the shoes that people want to buy. If nobody is buying the prototypes, they don't need to produce them.

AI is already producing marketing copy, audiobooks, paintings, and similar works that are difficult to distinguish from those produced by humans. If they're difficult to distinguish from humans now, they'll be difficult to distinguish from the masters in the future.

To be clear, I do not support AI taking the place of humans. As I mentioned earlier, the role of humans is to create and to think. It is to focus on the why and how. But if the what is clear, the role of technology is to produce the what, especially if it can produce it faster and better than we can.

We can get a glimpse into the future of work through the concept of decentralized autonomous organizations (DAOs), a concept used in blockchain.

The person who created the most wealth in the last five years is Changpeng Zhao—commonly known as CZ—founder of Binance, which is the largest exchange for crypto, Bitcoin, and other similar currencies. He started out as an engineer in Beijing. One day he had an idea for a business that he knew would be the future, but he had no money. He and his wife sold their house and put all their money into his company. Five years later, he is worth $75 billion.

Binance is a DAO, with thousands of employees all around the world. The entire company is run by code, where there are many small units in various countries, and most people, when they communicate internally, use nicknames. For example, Sonia would not identify herself as "Sonia" but as "Red Sheep." Many employees do not even know the full list of people who work for the company.

This example is an extreme one, but I believe the most successful companies in the future will be those who automate as much as possible, like DAOs do. Eventually, you won't need to hire people to manage processes, because your smart employees will have created the code, smart contracts, and other automated systems to take care of repeatable processes like hiring and onboarding.

This is how the Atomic Scaling method of 3P3R can be for everyone. It's ultimately about creating a culture of prediction, which will allow your teams to serve more people, fulfill your mission, and scale your impact.

CASE STUDY: VALVE

Valve Corporation is a video game developer, publisher, and digital distribution company headquartered in the Seattle, Washington, area of the United States. They developed the distribution platform Steam as well as hit games like Counter-Strike, Half-Life, Portal, Day of Defeat, Left 4 Dead, Team Fortress, and the Dota series.

Since its inception, Valve has been growing about 50 percent per year and has a much higher revenue and profitability ratio per employee than Apple, Google, or Microsoft.

In 2012, Valve had approximately 250 employees and was worth over $3 billion, which made it the most profitable company per employee in the United States.[48]

Valve generates more internet traffic than most countries right now.

So how does a Seattle-based company of 360 people, similar in size to Supercell today, achieve so much?

When designing a company to be the most profitable company in the world, here are the key playbook principles Valve lives by.

First, *hire the best talent and reward them accordingly*. As we discussed in the People chapter, the movement towards outsourcing, or trying to find the lowest cost employees you can, is precisely the opposite of what you should be doing. Valve finds the best talent in the world and more than covers their cost with the resulting profit. (See the EPIC employees section in Chapter 1.)

The second principle is to *remain independent*. Reduce the need for the approval process from the board, managers, and investors. If you make a wrong decision, fix that problem rather than arguing about the pros and cons.

Third, *own your distribution channel* rather than trying to fit into someone else's distribution channel. Eliminate the source of noise between consumers and producers as much as you can.

Fourth, *eliminate hierarchies and titles*. Valve does not have management. They usually give the job of making other people more productive to younger people. Valve has no QA (Quality Assurance) department and no marketing department. Everybody at the company instead assumes that their job is to talk to customers outside of the company.

Valve's largest single room right now has about eighty people in it. All desks are on wheels and only have two contact points with the floor, so employees can easily move their desks and join a different group of people in about fifteen minutes. Some people are trying to build a desk more optimal for paired programming.

"Valve Handbook for New Employees" got leaked in 2012. It describes Valve's culture with great humor and illustrations, aka "a fearless adventure in knowing what to do when no one's there telling you what to do."[49]

VALVE'S KEY PLAYBOOK PRINCIPLES

- Get the best talent in the world, and reward them accordingly
- Remain independent
- Own your distribution channel
- Eliminate hierarchies and titles

SET A RHYTHM

Once you define your mission, users, and method, the final key step for your playbook is to set a rhythm of regular meetings to establish and reinforce your culture.

Why? Creating a playbook is not enough; you must regularly share your mission, users, and method with your team members if you want your playbook to drive your culture.

Also, establishing a rhythm provides a sense of safety for your team. If you've made the shift toward empowering your teams rather than controlling them, sometimes things can seem chaotic—especially if you're in startup mode. With regular meetings, your team knows that no matter how busy everyone gets, they can count on regular times to check in, ask questions, share ideas, and problem solve.

A rhythm also creates efficiency. Instead of interrupting your co-founder or co-worker every five minutes with a new idea, you can write down your ideas or questions and save them for the meeting you know will be coming up in three days, or twenty-four hours, or whatever your rhythm happens to be.

There are many different types of meetings or activities you could schedule to create a rhythm for your team, but to establish and reinforce your culture, the three most important are the following:

- a weekly founders' meeting
- a weekly informal meeting for team members
- a weekly all-hands meeting, where the CEO has an opportunity to reinforce the company's origin story and values

In my opinion, the *founders' meeting* is the most important. When Sheryl Sandberg was hired as Facebook's COO, she had one rule for founder Mark Zuckerberg: every Monday at 8:30, no matter how busy they were, they would meet together for one hour. There was no agenda and no rules beyond that one meeting.

No matter how busy you are as a founder, make time to meet regularly with your other founders or partners. You don't have to work together all the time, and you don't even need an agenda, but you do need to meet regularly.

Next is a weekly opportunity for *self-organized informal sharing* among team members for about two hours or so.

Many companies have happy hours, where there are drinks and chips and socializing, which tend to be organized by management or HR. But ideally, these weekly informal gatherings are self-organized and more organic.

For example, every Monday afternoon, team members at Riot Games in Santa Monica, California, gather and decide what topics they want to discuss or learn more about. Then they self-organize into groups of five, six, or seven to meet about each topic, whether it's hearing more about the new champion for their latest game, problem-solving about a technical issue, or sharing new ideas.

Another important weekly meeting is an *all-hands meeting*, which all employees attend either virtually or in person, including the CEO and founders. This is an opportunity for employees to ask questions, and for the CEO or founders to talk about the mission, the people they serve, and the company's origin story.

One French AI company I'm working with, Aleia, has an extraordinary origin story. When French president Emmanuel Macron wanted to create a French AI strategy, he gathered a famous mathematician, a few other experts, and the future CEO of Aleia, Antoine Couret. Aleia was born as a result of the French AI strategy created to solve three problems identified in the report produced by this group President Macron commissioned.

As a result of this strategy, France has now positioned itself globally in AI, which will have a significant effect on its industries and sovereignty as a nation.

Aleia now has thirty-five employees, and most of them have never heard this story! They had no idea the president of the country asked their CEO to come up with an AI strategy, and their company is essentially executing it, and improving the future of their country, as a result.

When we realized that, we added a rhythm of a weekly all-hands meeting, where at the beginning of every meeting, we share the origin story.

A consistent rhythm is a small key that opens large doors and helps you avoid big, big problems. It also makes running the company a lot easier. When I was an entrepreneur and CEO, I didn't know anything about rhythm. I had meeting after meeting and urgency after urgency, but I didn't realize that the faster we grew, the more crises we were having because more and more employees didn't know our mission, our values, or our story. We weren't sharing them on a regular basis.

Also, as a company grows, CEOs tend to spend less time with employees, which means CEOs have less impact on the hiring process. If the team doesn't have a strong playbook about their mission, users, and method, and if they do not consistently hear the same origin story again and again, they will make up their own story and may end up hiring people who are not the best fit for the company. As a result, the company may become very different than what the CEO or founding team intended. But if you are regularly sharing your mission and origin story with your employees every Friday, when they are starting new projects, hiring new people, or talking to the media, they will soon be able to tell your company's story as well as or even better than you would.

If you feel like your culture isn't strong enough to justify regular meetings, establishing a rhythm is exactly what will make it stronger. It's a lot like going to the gym. Even if you don't feel strong enough or in shape enough to go to the gym, if you keep going week after week, you will get stronger. If you don't go to the gym, you will only get weaker.

It's the same with your culture. If you have a rhythm of daily, weekly, or monthly meetings, your culture will get stronger. If you do nothing, it won't.

For example, another company I invested in was growing fast and had smart, talented people. The problem was nobody knew they existed. When we first began working together, they said they didn't have enough news to justify a regular news cycle. I encouraged them to create a rhythm where they would release news every week, no matter what. It didn't matter if their story was picked up by TechCrunch or VentureBeat or the *LA Times*; at the very least it was going to be on Newswire, and it would improve their search engine optimization and ranking.

Just a few weeks after beginning this rhythm, they discovered they actually did have enough news for a weekly news cycle. After following their rhythm consistently, their company began to rank higher on Google, and investors started cold calling them to schedule meetings.

As you schedule your rhythm and practice again and again, it will become second nature. And your culture will get stronger.

What is one new meeting or practice you can schedule to establish or reinforce your culture's mission, values, and origin story?

Finally, you don't have to wait until you're sure about your MUM or your rhythm before you start writing things down. Writing down your mission and values early is important, even if you have just a few people in your company.

In fact, one of co-founder Ilkka Paananen's self-proclaimed biggest personal mistakes at Supercell is that it took him too long to define and write down Supercell's values. Among their founding team of six, Ilkka felt the team was completely clear about the culture they wanted to build. Two years and forty hires later, he finally wrote down their key values. "I didn't do it sooner," Ilkka explained, "partly because putting together a memo or culture deck sounded like a very corporate thing to do, but mostly because I was just so busy doing other stuff (that felt more important and urgent at the time)."

But when he attended a meeting where someone was talking about "responsibility" (one of Supercell's values) in a completely different way than Ilkka and the founders thought of it, he realized nothing was *more* important than writing down the company's values.

As Ilkka says, "Culture is defined by the hardest decisions." And if values are what guide teams in making those decisions, it's very important to make sure everyone is defining them in the same way!

Even though it took a lot of time, Ilkka met individually with every single Supercellian to ask them what they thought the company values were. He summarized them in a few slides, made sure they were consistent with the company they wanted to build, and now had a culture document the company revisits every year or two. "This was a huge effort, but well worth it," Ilkka says. "I just wish I had done it when there were only six of us."[50]

So don't wait to write your playbook. Start today, share it with your team, and iterate fast!

GAME ON: PLAYBOOK

- ☐ **Define your mission.** What is your moonshot? What ignites such passion in you and your team that would be worth trying and failing at?
- ☐ **Define your users with the BRAW Framework.**
  - ◦ What big total addressable market can you serve?
  - ◦ Who do you relate to?
  - ◦ Who do you have access to?
  - ◦ Who do you want to serve?
  - ◦ What group of people meets all four of these criteria? These are your BRAW users.
- ☐ **Define your method.** How can you begin using prediction as part of your core method in your company? (You'll learn more about this in Part Two.)
- ☐ **Set a rhythm.** What weekly meeting or activity can you schedule now to provide structure to your company and strengthen your culture?

Part 2

THE 3RS: REVENUE, REACH, AND RETENTION

Chapter 4

REVENUE

In the 2000s, I was living in North America. Most people were still using phone landlines back then (including me), and long-distance calls were very expensive—especially international calls. The cheapest way to call my mother in France on a landline was to use Skype, a new VoIP service, and charge my credit card for the calls.

However, Skype would allow us to make international calls for free if we were willing to talk to each other through our computers. It seemed incredible that a company could offer free long-distance calls when virtually every other telephone provider charged so much. All I had to do was convince my mom to download Skype and talk to me through her computer instead of a landline.

Luckily, I was able to convince her, and we were able to call each other for free and talk as long as we wanted. It was a clear win for us—but how could it be a win for Skype?

Skype was a famous early pioneer in what is now called the freemium revenue model—meaning their primary service was free. It was founded in 2003, and just two years later in 2005, Skype was acquired by eBay for $2.6 billion. In just two years, Skype managed to get to fifty million registered users by 2005 and increased more than ten-fold to more than 600 million just five years later. In 2011, it was bought by Microsoft for $8.5 billion.

With a business value of billions of dollars, obviously Skype was creating a lot of revenue. How could it create so much revenue when it was giving its product away for free?

Hint: It took more than just a free product.

In this chapter, we'll cover what the freemium model is (and what it is not), why the most successful gaming companies use this revenue model, and how you can create it for your business.

CASE STUDY: SKYPE

Skype was created by accident. The company, which was not called Skype at that time, had run out of money and was about to go bankrupt. The engineers didn't know what to do, and they needed to talk to their boss, Niklas Zennstrom, right away.

The only problem was that Niklas was in Estonia while they were in Sweden. Instead of making an expensive international call, they decided to try making a phone call using the open-source peer-to-peer technology they had developed. They discovered they were able to make a phone call from Sweden to Estonia for free.

At first, Niklas thought, *Okay, that's pretty cool—thanks for saving the company some money.* Then he realized, *Wait a minute—this could be our business.* So a whole new business was born because one of the engineers felt bad the company was going bankrupt.

Later, Niklas sold Skype three times: he sold it first to eBay, then he bought it back himself, and finally to Microsoft. He also invested in Rovio and Supercell, two of the most successful gaming companies in Finland. And he was an investor in one of my first companies in China, which was his first investment in China. Since then, he has become a very famous investor in Europe with his own investment firm, Atomico.

Two reasons why Skype could be offered for free were (1) the technology had already been created, and (2) the cost of a new user was almost zero. That's a key differentiator for the free-mium model: your product should be free and simple to set up.

Today, many other services offer free phone calls to their users, such as Facebook Messenger, Viber, WhatsApp, Instagram chat, and Telegram. But none of them offer a truly freemium model, as you will see later in this chapter.

WHAT IS THE FREEMIUM REVENUE MODEL?

Traditionally, as Josh Kaufman states in his book *The Personal MBA*, if you want to increase the revenue of your business, you can:

1. Increase the number of customers
2. Increase the average transaction size
3. Increase the frequency of transactions per customer
4. Increase your prices[51]

To increase revenue using this model, traditional companies usually have to qualify their customers, because not every customer is the right customer. As Kaufman explains, "Some customers will sap your time, energy, and resources without providing the results that you're looking for. If you're spending a lot of energy serving customers who don't come in often, have a low average transaction size, don't spread the word, and complain about the price, it doesn't make sense to attract more of those customers."

As a result, according to Kaufman, business owners should focus their efforts on serving their ideal customers who, in contrast, visit often, spend more, spread the word, and pay a premium for their services. "The more ideal customers you can attract," Kaufman concludes, "the better your business."[52]

While the above is all true, believe it or not, there are five other ways to increase your revenue:

1. Dramatically increase the number of customers by at least 10x
2. Decrease your lowest transaction size *and* increase your highest transaction size by segmenting your offers to different customer types (usually called *minnows*, *dolphins*, and *whales*)
3. Dramatically increase the spending capability per customer
4. Increase the frequency of transactions and loyalty per customer
5. Lower *and* raise your prices, according to customer segment

These are the principles followed by a freemium model, and which gaming companies have used to their immense success.

The gaming industry's impressive growth and size came from the paradigm shift from the traditional "pay-to-play" model to the "free-to-pay" model.

Before, gaming revenue was calculated by multiplying the unit price by the number of units sold. Games typically sold for USD 69.

League of Legends and Clash of Clans, both free-to-play and both phenomenal successes, caused the rest of the industry to realize that free-to-play was the most powerful revenue model. Now, most gaming companies embrace this model.

Free-to-play video games are games in which players have access to a fully functional game for free, and they access additional features and benefits through microtransactions.

In the gaming industry today, most revenue comes from the purchase of in-game items, the most common being weapons, cars, character outfits, and skins. With the rise of online advertising, in addition to these microtransactions, a complementary way to generate revenue is to integrate advertisements into the game.

Because revenue comes from the purchase of very low-cost digital items, some assume the gaming industry is not making significant revenue and therefore do not take the industry seriously.

Yet the free-to-play model has become one of the most profitable revenue models. For instance, out of League of Legends' $20 billion of revenue, most comes from selling in-game items, skins, and League of Legends (LoL) champions. Seattle-based PC game company Valve and Shenzhen-based mobile gaming company Tencent both follow the free-to-play model.

Although the world (of revenue) may be flat with pay-to-play, it is drastically dynamic with a freemium revenue model.

According to Valve co-founder and CEO Gabe Newell, the free-to-play model generally yields a 10x audience growth rate and a 3x revenue growth rate when the revenue model includes both advertising and microtransactions.

"By adopting free to play, audience size goes up by 10x.

"Gross revenue typically goes up by 3x."

—GABE NEWELL

You've heard it said that the more you give, the more you will receive. The freemium model is that principle in action. The world of haves and have nots is coming to an end. The future of revenue is to serve the people with purpose-driven businesses.

Forget about those who can afford you and those who can't. Serve the people—the rich, the poor, and everyone in between. Adopt a freemium model.

WHAT FREEMIUM IS NOT

Freemium does *not* simply mean having free products. For example, Facebook Messenger, WhatsApp, and Google products like Gmail and Google Calendar are free to use, but they do not follow a freemium model. They make their money from advertising. To use the famous quote, if you don't pay, you are the product. These companies are not selling you anything because you are the product. The more time you spend using their products, the more money they generate from advertising.

Also, free products do not necessarily make great freemium products. It's not uncommon for startups to build a great free product and then say they'll take care of monetization later on. That's typically a recipe for failure, at least when it comes to revenue.

Why? The main reason is that when you build a freemium product, you build the product around the monetization mechanism based on expected usage. Rather than seeing freemium as a way of monetizing your customers, think of freemium as a way of acquiring them. Offering them a free product is a way of putting them into your sales funnel with the hopes of acquiring them as paying users.

If you add monetization later, you might become profitable after years and years of changing your products. But you probably won't enjoy the ride. You'll create a much smoother ride for yourself if you plan your monetization model from the beginning, to include paywalls, user segmentation, monetization lifecycle, and a sales funnel. We'll talk more about this in the section on monetization later in the chapter and in Chapter 5 on Reach.

Finally, the freemium model is not the fastest way to become profitable in the short term. As we mentioned in the Playbook chapter, prediction must be part of your method, no matter what product you create. You should always be testing your working hypothesis of who your users are, how you will monetize them, and what you want the customer lifecycle and funnel to look like. And as you learned in the Prediction chapter, that means you need a set of hypotheses you can measure, and you need to be able to iterate over and over again until you find a hypothesis that consistently yields a customer lifetime value that's greater than the customer acquisition cost.

That means planning and testing your monetization model will take time. Your first version probably won't be amazing. You might underestimate how many free users it takes to convert to paying, or the challenge of engaging or retaining your users long term, or the runway it takes to reach profitability. That's okay; just keep iterating.

The truth is the freemium model usually takes much longer to reach profitability than the traditional premium business model. Equity financing (angels and VCs) can help you bridge the gap, but not everyone has that opportunity or wants to do that—and not every venture capitalist will want to help you do that. Very few venture capitalists truly understand freemium economics. For example, many are afraid of the "hit-driven" aspect of the gaming industry and their capacity to judge a team, so most VCs tend to ignore gaming as a whole. Those who invest prefer proven teams or teams with games that already show reliable traction.

Nevertheless, despite these difficulties, you probably already know plenty of businesses (in addition to Skype) that succeeded with freemium. Here are a few. Note how many began within the gaming industry.

- **Evernote**, a note-taking app with over 225 million users worldwide, is not very "social" or "viral," yet it keeps growing.[53] It is an excellent example of a service or product whose value to users increases over time, which you will learn more about later. The more notes you create, the more difficult it is to leave the service.
- **LinkedIn**, a social network for businesses, is another classic freemium network effects organization (another principle we will discuss below). The more people in your network

join the service, the more valuable it becomes to you. Billionaire LinkedIn founder and legendary investor Reid Hoffman (sometimes called the "oracle of Silicon Valley" and creator of blitzscaling) has invested in many gaming companies, such as Zynga and Kongregate. Hoffman was also an early investor in Facebook and organized the first meeting between Mark Zuckerberg and Peter Thiel, his former partner at PayPal, who made the initial $500,000 angel investment in Facebook. Later on, Facebook made social gaming possible, which fueled the free-to-play gaming revolution.

- **Discord** was created by accident, much like Skype (see case study in Chapter 3). Jason Citron was the founder of the gaming company Hammer & Chisel, whose first game, Fates Forever, was released in 2014. Although Fates Forever was not financially successful, it did yield an incredibly profitable insight. While the game was being developed, Citron noticed that his teams were having difficulty collaborating with the currently available VoIP software. He then developed an internal VoIP solution that became Discord. As of July 2019, it has been used by more than 250 million people.[54]

- Similarly to Discord, **Slack** was also born in a gaming studio before becoming a standalone communication service. The original name of Slack, co-founded by Stewart Butterfield, was Tiny Speck. While Slack is one of the most popular real-time collaboration apps and platforms today, Tiny Speck's first product was the computer game Glitch, and Slack was an internal tool used for its development.[55] Slack is now listed on NASDAQ with a market capitalization of USD 18 billion as of July 2020.

- Before Slack, Stewart Butterfield co-founded a company called Ludicorp, which initially developed a massively multiplayer online role-playing game (MMORG) called Game

Neverending. Although Game Neverending failed to launch, Ludicorp's next product was a photo-sharing website called **Flickr**—which they sold to Yahoo.[56]

The freemium model is probably the best and the most powerful business model right now on Earth. Are you beginning to see the possibilities for your own business?

If so, you may be wondering, *If it takes more than a free product, what exactly does it take to create a great freemium business?*

ATOMIC SCALING IKIGAI

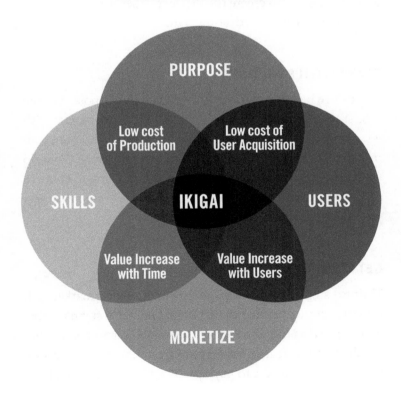

In this chapter, we will take a deeper look at what I call the *ikigai of freemium*. If you're not familiar with the term *ikigai*, it is a Japanese concept with no real direct translation in English. Ikigai embodies the idea of happiness in living. It's all about balance. If we apply this concept to the freemium model, the ikigai of freemium has seven steps:

1. Start with purpose.
2. Get tons of free users.
3. Get users to stick around.
4. Create a service or product whose value increases with time.
5. Keep cost per user low.
6. Get the skills to create the product or service.
7. Create a clear monetization plan.

START WITH PURPOSE

The future belongs to businesses driven by purpose. So, the first step of creating a freemium model is to reconnect with your purpose—or, as we called it in the previous chapter, your mission. So, remind yourself: What's your mission? What do you value most? What gets you up in the morning to come to work—not in least mode, but beast mode? Make sure whatever you create is aligned with your purpose.

GET TONS OF FREE USERS

The next step is to make sure you are addressing a market with tons of users. Remember the BRAW model: the B stands for big, as in *big total addressable market*. Freemium is a numbers game. For the first few years, an average of 1 to 5 percent of your total user base will convert to paying, so you need a huge addressable market for 1 to 5 percent to create the revenue you want. After ten years or so, if you become really good at what you do, your conversion percentage may be much higher. The true monopolies that dominate the market can hit 40 or 45 percent. But for at least the first few years, expect 1 to 5 percent of your user base to convert.

In the case of gaming, if you choose the freemium model, we typically say "don't go for a niche game" or a game that would appeal to a very small portion of the user base. For example, if you were doing a shooter game, the realistic military-type games like Counter-Strike or Call of Duty are much more popular than science-fiction shooter games, so you'd probably choose to develop a realistic-type game—until, of course, proven wrong by the market.

What service or product would appeal to the largest number of your users so you can have a big total addressable market?

GET USERS TO STICK AROUND

The holy grail metric of freemium is retention. We'll talk much more about retention later, but for now, if you're creating a freemium model, you need to make sure your users will stick around.

How? One way is to create a product or service your user wants to use as often as possible.

I want you to think very deeply about this one when you design the delivery. Start thinking outside the box right now. The key is to listen to what customers really want. Remember Justine

Musk's response to how to become a billionaire: you must create what people really want, not just what you want to make.

To design (or refine) a service your users will want to use as often as possible, ask yourself the following questions:

1. Does your service or product solve a one-time problem, or a recurring problem?

If it's a one-time problem, you'll pretty much be forgotten after a minute or two. Freemium works best with a recurring problem.

2. If it's a recurring problem, how often does your user have this problem: daily, weekly, monthly, quarterly, or yearly?

The more often someone uses your service, the better. Typically, daily is best.

If you're already solving a yearly or quarterly problem, freemium may not be the best model for your product. If you're solving a monthly problem, as in the case of Airbnb, freemium could work, but it may not be ideal. If you're solving a weekly problem, freemium is a good choice. And if you're solving a daily problem, it's perfect.

3. If your user will be using your service daily, how long will a session last?

If you have too many steps in your tutorial or onboarding process, for example, your session may take too long, and your users will click away.

Even more important is your download time. If it takes more than three seconds to get to the tutorial, most people will simply quit. Gaming companies are very good at download time right now, but most traditional companies ignore it. They rely on third-party or design agencies who create flashy intros, fancy logos, and very high-quality videos. The creative director from the big agency charging millions of dollars will do a very good job. But because many companies don't measure user engagement, they will not know that most of their customers are not waiting the four or five or ten seconds it takes for their app or program to load, and they have essentially wasted their money.

When you test an ad or an app, pay attention to download time. Most people click away after three seconds if they're not already interested.

4. Do your users need to use other products or services to effectively use your product or service?

If your customers are using other products or services when they're using your product or service, not only do they have an opportunity to get distracted and forget to return, your competitor has an opportunity to create a similar product or service to yours, so your customer has no need to return to you again. Remember that Slack and Discord were developed as in-house communication services when external communication services weren't exactly what their customers needed.

Also, many services are offered through a platform owned by another company, which offers many opportunities for your users to get distracted from your service, and to find a competitor who might offer a better service than you do.

For example, rather than relying on competitor platforms like Microsoft Xbox and Sony PlayStation, Valve created their own gaming platform called Steam.

Are there ways to meet your customer's need for other products and services by developing those products and services yourself, perhaps through your own ecosystem?

5. How many days will your users use your service: one day, seven days, thirty days, ninety days, 180 days, 360 days, two years, three years, five years?

In the gaming industry, you see these graphs a lot:

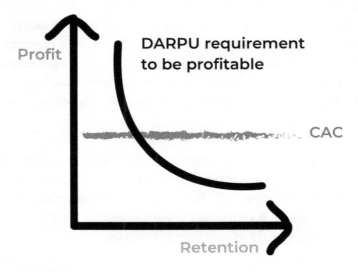

Typical Daily Average Revenue per User (DARPU) required to be profitable
(CAC = customer acquisition cost)

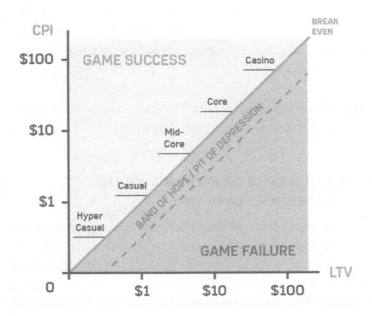

Every industry has its own benchmarks for profitability and retention, and you probably already know those benchmarks for your industry. For example, on what day does a user become profitable? If your users are still using your service after seven days, are they more likely to stay for 180 days? How long do they need to use your service to be more likely to stay for one year or more?

Typically, for software as a service (SaaS) businesses or similar freemium businesses, you want users to stick around for at least six months, because that's how long it takes to become profitable. For games, it can be much shorter, because after three to seven days, you are usually already profitable.

Also, in both the gaming and SaaS industries, the companies that can best predict retention and revenue have a competitive edge, as they can be more aggressive with their user acquisition spend and get more users faster. They don't mind waiting six months to get their money back if they're virtually certain they're going to get it.

What are the significant profitability and retention benchmarks for your industry, both offline and online?

CREATE A SERVICE OR PRODUCT WHOSE VALUE INCREASES OVER TIME

Another way to increase user stickiness is to create a product or service whose value increases over time—where the more often someone uses it, the more valuable it becomes to them. Also, the more people who use it, the more valuable your service becomes for everyone else.

In the gaming industry, examples include multiplayer games like World of Warcraft, where players invest tons of time and energy in building up their characters and making friends and alliances. The more time they invest in the game, the more the value of that game increases.

To create value that increases over time, there are two key factors you can leverage: *inventory* and *connections*.

Inventory typically refers to data. Think of Evernote, the note-taking app, where the more notes you enter, the stickier the product becomes. Think of Spotify, the music streaming service, where the more playlists you create and share, the more valuable it becomes to you. The more playlists you create, the more engaged you are, and the more often you return to the service. (For more about Spotify, see their case study below.)

"The more memories users store in Evernote, the more invested they become."

—PHIL LIBIN, FOUNDER OF EVERNOTE

Connections refers to the number of people in your network who also use the service, so the more people you know using the service, the more valuable the service is to you. From a business perspective, when a user has a vested interest in getting their entire network to use the product or service, this is known as the *network effect*. Think LinkedIn, Skype, Facebook, and any multiplayer game.

The more people you know use the service, the better the service gets for you as the user. When my mom joined Skype, the service became more valuable to me because I now got free international calls.

This is also why it can be very difficult for players to leave a multiplayer game: they have invested a lot in their clan, meaning they have made a lot of friends in the game. After four or five years of playing, they may find the game boring, but they continue playing to stay connected with their friends around the world.

In contrast, if your service's value six months from now will be the same as it is today—for example, if you facilitate users' purchase of a product through an online interface—you're most likely not designing the right product for your users. It will be too easy for competition to lower the price or add features and benefits, causing your people to drop out and churn.

How can you increase your users' value over time?

CASE STUDY: SPOTIFY

When it comes to the freemium model, Spotify is one of the biggest conversion-to-pay success stories today. At the time of this writing, Spotify, founded in 2006 by Swedish entrepreneurs Daniel Ek and Martin Lorentzon, is valued at $42 billion on the NASDAQ. It has 165 million paying subscribers and 365 million monthly active users, which means their monthly versus paying ratio is 45 percent. The other 55 percent who are not paying are being monetized with ads.

I knew Daniel and some of Spotify's early founders, investors, and employees, and I remember suggesting that Niklas Zennstrom, the founder of Skype, invest in Spotify. At that time, Niklas didn't want to invest in Spotify because he believed it would be too difficult to convert users into paying users. (He ended up investing in a competitor of Spotify that nearly went bankrupt.) Within a decade, Daniel and the Spotify team had the 45 percent conversion ratio it has today. What seemed impossible at that time, even to the founder of Skype, became one of the biggest successful freemium businesses at that time.

I helped Spotify to launch in France with a few introductions to the local press, and one night I was with Daniel, Shak, Niklas, Sean Parker, and a bunch of other guys in a club in Paris. Spotify was quite small then, and we were excited about the possibilities. At that time, I was probably the number one user in France, because I got the account before they launched, and I was already using it every day.

"I really love Spotify," I told Daniel. "I've literally used it every day since the beta launch."

"Oh, thank you," Daniel said. "Do you have any recommendations?"

"Actually, I have one recommendation," I admitted. "You have a huge library of songs, and you have the API ready." (That means other developers can access the Spotify platform and create all kinds of additional services.) "How about making the API and Spotify platform more obvious, to encourage more developers to use it?" I was a developer myself, and I thought more people needed to know about this possibility.

Daniel, a very calm Swedish guy, looked at me and said, "Actually, we're going to close down the API and platform access to developers."

"Really?" I asked, surprised. "But why?"

Then Daniel told me something you should be familiar with by now. "It's all about the playbook."

Okay, I've heard this before, I thought. "Tell me more."

"It's all about the playbook," he said again. "We realized we have two core strengths. The first is we need to have the largest catalog of songs on the internet available for free.

"The second is that we need to have the songs instantly accessible without buffering time." Buffering time is the time it takes for the song to start on your computer or phone after you click on it. (This sounded very boring to me at the time.)

And then he told me, "Everything else we are de-prioritizing and saying no."

Remember what Steve Jobs said: Focus is about saying no.

Spotify now has 70 million tracks, which is the largest collection of songs available legally for free on the internet. And there's pretty much no buffering time, or very, very little, in 178 countries.

Last time I saw Daniel, he was visiting Beijing. We had lunch together and discussed that Tencent was the largest investor in Spotify, owning about 10 percent. He told me more about how they negotiated the deal. Tencent had offered a lower valuation than other investors in China, but Spotify partnered with Tencent because it owns the largest catalog of Chinese songs worldwide. And if Tencent was an investor in Spotify, they would have access to Tencent's collections of songs in Chinese.

It's all about the playbook.

As an aside, Sean Parker, the co-founder of Napster, was one of the guys with us in that club in Paris. Napster was the first and largest completely illegal file-sharing service available worldwide. Because it was illegal, it was shut down, and he was ordered to pay billions of dollars in fines. At that time, he was 19 years old. By the time he was 24, he was the founding president of Facebook as well as an investor in Facebook.

That night in Paris, he had just become an investor in Spotify, and he was very happy. He was dancing like there was no tomorrow, because he knew they were going to do it right this time.

About two years later, Spotify discovered a key predictor of retention: the more playlists you created early, the more likely you were to return to the platform and ultimately become a paying user. So just as Daniel in the very early days focused on having the largest catalog of songs for free and no buffering time, they changed their focus almost exclusively to getting you to create playlists as early as possible.

One day at a conference, when Sean Parker was excitedly explaining the power of that prediction, he said that the moment a user creates a playlist, "we've got you by the balls." Of course, this was not a very nice way to say it, but he was excited. They had discovered that the one thing that predicted whether people would stick to the platform was the playlist the users created themselves.

Remember the discussion about inventory and connection above: Spotify had figured out that connection—in their case, the number of friends users followed—was not dramatically increasing their retention. But with inventory (i.e., playlists), "we got you by the balls." In fact, I am listening to an Atomic Scaling playlist I created on Spotify as I write this.

The power of prediction plus the power of the playbook equals exponential revenue.

KEEP COST PER USER LOW

In addition to all of the above, you will also want to keep your cost per user relatively low. But the key is to use a broader and more dynamic definition of cost, rather than the traditional model of only looking at the profitability of the project.

Should a product be priced above its cost per user? Usually yes, but sometimes no. Let's take a more detailed look at what it means to keep your cost per user low.

The two costs to consider are the *cost of acquisition* and the *cost of production*. The cost of acquisition is typically 30 percent of your overall cost; it can be even higher. We'll talk more about cost of acquisition in the next chapter, but here's the important point: the cost of production does not just include the initial cost of production. That's important, but what matters most is *the cost of production of an additional unit.*

"It costs us virtually nothing for a new user to join the Skype network."
—NIKLAS ZENNSTROM, FOUNDER OF SKYPE

For example, I'm on the board of a French AI company, and it cost millions of dollars to develop their initial product. At one point, their project was showing a negative 60 percent profitability. But their margin for additional customers beyond the first customer is extremely high. It doesn't make sense to look at profitability per project if the project requires developing new technology. In this case, they can think of their revenue as financing most of their research and development (R&D) costs. The most important metric for them is their cost of production of an additional unit.

Also, with this more dynamic definition of cost, one way to keep your overall cost per user low is to keep your operating costs relatively low. One very effective way to do that is to keep your team small and to use the reverse pyramid of power, as we discussed in the chapters on People and Prediction. This can save you a lot of overhead costs on hiring and managing employees.

What can you do to lower your cost per unit, using this more dynamic definition of cost?

GET THE SKILLS TO CREATE THE SERVICE OR PRODUCT

By now, you probably have an idea of a service or product that provides something tons of your users want (ideally daily), whose value increases over time, and that has a low cost per user (when viewed dynamically). Here's the next question: Do you have the skills to create this product or service?

Begin by listing all the steps needed to create and deliver your service or product. Then list all the skills those steps require. Do you and your team already have those skills? How can you access the skills you need? If the skills have to do with the "what," which is done the same way every time, consider using technology to automate these steps. If the skills have to do with the "why" or "how," that's what people are for. Remember the 2.5x Valve rule from the People chapter: be willing to invest in the best talent available so each team member can serve as many users as possible.

If you have little to no money available for hiring, you may be wondering, *How can I afford the best talent?* That brings us to the next step: your monetization plan.

CREATE A CLEAR MONETIZATION PLAN

The final question to achieve the ikigai of freemium: Do you have a clear monetization plan?

A clear monetization plan means you have a set of hypotheses, you are able to measure them, and you can iterate quickly based on the results. Remember the pendulum framework from the Prediction chapter.

Your hypothesis, in this case, should include paywalls, which means you should carefully choose when to introduce certain paid features in the user experience and at what price. (When and how to introduce discounted prices will be discussed further in Chapter 6 when we cover retention and live ops.) Also, segment users based on usage and revenue; they won't behave the same and will react differently to your offering, so stop treating everyone the same in your messaging and marketing. When it comes to monetization lifecycle and funnel, envision the ideal lifecycle from free sign-up to activation to first-time purchase to upsell—and how users flow between multiple paid offerings.

Remember, you're not designing a free product and adding monetization later. Monetization is part of the product already.

Gaming companies have taken the monetization of "free" to a whole new scientific level, generating billions of dollars per game. Games franchises, if well operated, can last for decades.

Here's how it works. To build a freemium product, where monetization is built in from the beginning, you must first segment your customers.

The traditional company uses this revenue formula, which is directly correlated to how much you can raise your prices:

Revenue = number of customers × average transaction size × average transaction frequency per customer

$$R = c \times ats \times atf$$

In contrast, gaming companies use this Atomic Scaling revenue formula:

$$R = M(c \times ats \times atf) + D(c \times ats \times atf) + W(c \times ats \times atf)$$

In this equation, M, D, and W stand for the three standard customer segments, based on their current level of spending:

1. Minnows
2. Dolphins
3. Whales

How do I categorize my users based on spending behaviors?

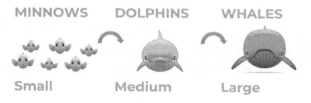

MINNOWS   DOLPHINS   WHALES

Small   Medium   Large

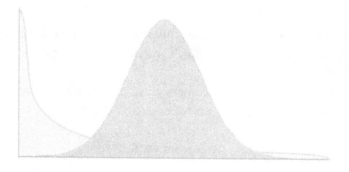

A minnow is a player who monetizes little to nothing. And that's okay. You want plenty of minnows entering your funnel, as you can gradually move them to become dolphins or whales, while they also actively contribute to community activity and recruitment of new members. Typically, a minnow will go for the cheapest offering available, from free to usually under $5.

A dolphin monetizes decently and is usually a more rational user. Dolphins appreciate the service and the community, and actively engage with it daily. They are happy with free and "normal to have" paid items in order to fully enjoy and participate in the game. Dolphins typically go for the mid-range offering and don't necessarily repeat their purchase often, if at all.

A whale constitutes the minority of the user base but often contributes most of the revenue. It is what other industries would call a VIP, or in China, a VVIP (Very Very Important Person). There is almost no limit on how much a whale can spend. The limitation in spending often comes from game design and poor community service rather than the whale's ability or interest in spending. While you often see revenue graphed as a normal distribution in the traditional model, when you're using a freemium model, it's very much a power law curve in terms of the volume and revenue you generate from these categories of users.

In a balanced freemium model, minnows represent 65 percent of your volume and generate 20 percent of your revenue. Dolphins, or your average users, represent 30 percent of your volume and around 40 percent of your revenue. Whales might represent only 5 percent of your volume but 40 percent of your total revenue. In fact, it's not uncommon for the gaming industry to see 10 percent of your user base represent 80 percent of your revenue.

How users contribute to	Volume	vs	Revenue
Minnows ▶	65%		20%
Dolphins ▶	30%		40%
Whales ▶	5%		40%

As an example, a minnow in the transportation industry would typically be a free rider. A dolphin would be a car buyer. A dolphin would own a car or a maximum of two and would not necessarily interact much with a transportation community or buy additional services.

A whale would be way beyond even the most luxurious car company's premium users. A whale's spending would not be limited by how many cars one can own. A whale's spending would only be determined by how much one can contribute to the community based on their spending ability and desire.

In a game, top whales are usually clan leaders, providing their troops the best equipment to win in-game challenges against other clans. One could easily see that happening in the transportation industry in a well-designed community and business model.

In fact, as you're thinking about your monetization strategy, think in terms of creating an ecosystem or economy. Here's how Gabe Newell of Valve explains it:

> On the surface, [a] free-to-play game sounds like a horrible idea. I['m going to] give my product away for free? Most people just sort of stop right there and go, "Okay, that's, that's horrible." But in a free-to-play game, what you're really doing is you're creating a lot of goods that are related to a status and affinity and hierarchy. You're creating a whole bunch of goods there, and the marginal or the incremental value of an audience member is greater than the incremental cost of making that person an audience member. So typically what we see with the free-to-play game, which on the surface sounds like suicide, is that your audience size goes up by a factor of ten, and your gross revenue goes up by a factor of three. [But] since your incremental cost of another audience member is fairly small—just the cost of distributing those bits to those customers—your profitability tends to increase a lot more than a factor of three.[57]

One final word about whales. In the West, there can be a negative view of whales, or the people who seem to have no limit on what they are willing to spend. Some might even consider the freemium business model, which encourages high spending, to be an unethical business model. For example, if someone spends $1 or even up to $200 in a game, most Westerners think that's already too much to spend on a "free" game. If someone spends a thousand dollars, that person is clearly addicted. And then if someone spends $10,000 in a game, well, clearly a kid stole a credit card from his parents.

But in the East and the Middle East, the whales are not spending the money on themselves. They are spending the money for the people in their group.

For example, if you go to a restaurant in France, you might have five people around the table, and when you receive the bill, everyone will contribute the exact amount of money their individual meal costs. In America, you might also have five people at the table, and you might ask for separate checks, or get one check and split the bill evenly.

But in China, you have twenty people around at the table with two or three whales, and those whales are going to fight over who gets to pay for the whole table.

Similarly, the whales in gaming are usually not spending the money for them. They are spending the money for their group. If you have money, you are happy to let others benefit from it. The gaming whales in China aren't the rich kids from Beijing or Shanghai; they're the rich kids from cities or towns you've never heard of, typically in the west of China. For them, spending on gaming is their way to connect with friends around the country. The typical gaming whale is a fourteen-year-old flying around in his private jet, picking up friends all around the country so they can go back to his house in his small town to train together.

As Gabe Newell has said, we have to stop thinking of spending as consumption. Spending is not consumption. In the East or Middle East, we might say whales spend for social status, while in the more individualistic United States, we might say impact. Either way, the bigger purpose can be service to society or your group. If you or your family has money, there's a drive to serve or to give back to your community, your university, or your group.

The common denominator is service.

That's why your purpose as the founder of a freemium model must be very clear from the start. If your purpose is just to make money, the freemium model may not make sense. But if your purpose is mission driven, then your decisions will optimize for impact rather than profit alone. And if you're optimizing for impact, it makes sense to serve whales who have no limit on their spending, because they also have no limit on their impact.

Every time you face a tough decision, ask yourself, Am I optimizing for profit, or am I optimizing for impact? If you're not sure, go for impact every time—and you will make more profit. That's how Riot Games became so successful: they never optimized for revenue or profit; they always optimized for engagement, which led to retention, which led to greater profit. Again, we'll talk more about retention in Chapter 6.

So I don't believe a business model that encourages high spending is unethical. What I believe is unethical is a business model based on advertising, which takes over people's minds. Google's tagline used to be "Don't be evil." YouTube, which was bought by Google, is easily the dominant internet platform worldwide when it comes to music and video. But their revenue comes from advertising, which is designed to suck people's mind into the content and make choices against their better judgment. In terms of impact, I see this as a very negative impact.

TikTok and Facebook operate the same way. If we could create a social network based on the freemium model, I believe we would not have many of the problems we have right now in our political systems and democracies.

Who are the minnows, dolphins, and whales in your business, and how can you monetize your product or service for each segment?

Finally, for your monetization plan, the key measurement you're looking for is when customer lifetime value is greater than customer acquisition cost (LTV>CAC).

"Good unit economics is one where the startup can recoup its customer acquisition cost (CAC) on a net contribution margin basis during the first 6 months of operations. We also look for the startup to 3x its CAC in 18 months."

—FABRICE GRINDA, INVESTOR

When LTV>CAC, it's time to scale—which we'll cover in more detail in the next chapter.

When you adopt the freemium model, you'll start to become data driven, and the results can be magical.

You create your hypothetical model, you measure, and you iterate. And once you excel at operating your model, you will be able to predict almost to the dollar how much you're going to generate next Monday from this specific promotion. And you will be able to say, "Okay, if we choose that promotion versus this promotion, this is how much additional revenue we're going to generate." It's almost like someone is writing the game for you.

The freemium model shows us that the key to increasing revenue is to give more to more people. Be more generous—in your business as well as your personal life.

Deciding you want to give more to more people, rather than simply creating a free product and monetizing it later, will create a major shift in how you build your products and operate your business. It might sound easy, but it can be quite challenging for companies that have always focused on profit first. The truth is that you can make even more profit by offering more to more people.

The mindset shift from focusing on making money to focusing on serving more people (which happens to make more money) can take time. But don't get discouraged. If we are very clear about our own purpose, if we aren't distracted by what our competitors are doing, and if our intention is truly to give more to more people, then I believe we have a huge opportunity ahead of us, and the future becomes quite exciting!

GAME ON: REVENUE

☐ **Start with purpose.** Remind yourself of your mission and why you are creating this revenue model in the first place.

☐ **Get tons of free users.** What service or product would appeal to the largest number of your users so you can have a big total addressable market?

☐ **Get users to stick around.**
- Does your product or service solve a one-time problem, or a recurring problem? If it solves a one-time problem, is there a recurring problem you could solve for your ideal users?
- How can you solve your ideal users' recurring problem on a daily or weekly basis?
- How can you optimize your session or service time? Are you minimizing download time, if applicable?

- If your users must use other products and services to use your product or service, how might you develop those yourself, perhaps through your own ecosystem?
- What are the significant profitability and retention benchmarks for your industry, both offline and online? Create a hypothesis and prediction cycle to aim for these benchmarks.

☐ **Create a service or product whose value increases with time.**
  - How might you leverage the power of inventory, or personal data, in your product or service?
  - How might you leverage the power of connections, or the network effect, in your product or service?

☐ **Keep cost per user low.** How might you lower your cost per unit, using a dynamic definition of cost?

☐ **Get the skills to create the product or service.** What skills do you need to automate, develop, or hire for?

☐ **Create a clear monetization plan.**
  - Who are the minnows, dolphins, and whales in your business?
  - How can you monetize your product or service for each of these segments?
  - What are your free versus paid offers? Where are your paywalls?
  - What is your ideal monetization lifecycle and funnel, from free sign-up to activation to first-time purchase to upsell? How do users flow between multiple paid offerings?
  - Are you measuring to know when customer lifetime value is greater than customer acquisition cost (LTV>-CAC)? When LTV>CAC, it's time to scale.

Chapter 5

REACH

"Give a man a fish, and you feed him for a day. Teach a man to fish, and you feed him for a lifetime."

—COMMON PROVERB

You've probably been fishing at least once in your life. As a kid, I remember going fishing with my dad and my brother. Over the years, I've learned to approach business with the mindset of a fisherman.

I see two types of sales representatives in a company: the hunters and the fishermen. (I would also include CEOs in this group because they are typically the first sales representatives.)

The hunters wake up in the morning and go hunting for new clients. They see one potential lead, like a hunter sees a rabbit, and boom, they shoot. They give their sales pitch. Then they see another rabbit and boom, another sales pitch. And then some bird—bam, bam, bam—shots are going in every direction. They shoot everywhere, but at the end of the day, they feel like they haven't hit much. They managed to get maybe a few birds or rabbits, but it's never enough. They go to bed hungry and hope that tomorrow will be a better hunting day.

If you go to bed with this feeling of underachievement—especially if you're in a sales position—feeling like you didn't have enough hours during the day, or didn't kill enough birds or rabbits or clients, you might be a hunter.

Then there are the fishermen. They wake up with a smile on their face. They usually enjoy a sip of coffee before they check on their net from the previous day. They have already predicted how many fish or how many clients they will have caught during the night. They know that their net is getting stronger and stronger, meaning fish are not breaking free. They also know which part of the lake, or which part of the market on the internet, is a particularly good place to set their net. And usually, about midday, they may check out and go play with their kids for the rest of the afternoon. They go to bed hugging their spouse and giving thanks for another good day of fishing.

Which life do you want? Would you prefer to be the hunter or the fisherman? Personally, I would rather make a living fishing.

You can indeed choose to wake up in the morning with blood in your eyes and hunt down new clients. Or you can have a more systematic approach to sales, like a fisherman casting a net into the water.

I believe the time for hunting new clients is over—especially as the world moves online. You may know the biblical quote, "Follow me, and I will make you fishers of men." Let's spread the good news that we no longer have to be hunters. Let's become fishers of people's hearts by serving them better.

What does this mean in practical terms? It means don't focus on setting sales goals; focus on building a revenue-generating system.

"Traditional goal setting does not work in our culture of independent cells."

—ILKKA PAANANEN, FOUNDER OF SUPERCELL

As James Clear points out in *Atomic Habits* (no relation to this book!), our results have very little to do with the goals we set and almost everything to do with the system we follow.[58]

Most salespeople focus on the goal. A little bit like the hunter, they wake up anxious and say to themselves, "Oh my God, I need to reach my goals, I need to reach my goals." They focus too much on the goals and not enough on the system that will allow them to achieve the goals.

Results depend less on the goal you set than the system you follow. So don't focus on sales goals; focus on your sales system.

When people think of salespeople, they tend to think of the used car salesman, using all kinds of techniques to be better at closing. Or they think of Leonardo DiCaprio in the movie *The Wolf of Wall Street* when he says, "Sell me this pen."

The truth is the best salespeople are nothing like that. The best salespeople rely on relationships, offer 10x value, create offers they package differently for different customer segments, and build a better system.

So let's build a revenue-generating machine—a process, a system, and possibly a bit of technology that helps you attract leads, nurture them, and turn them into customers.

This machine is typically called a *sales funnel*. A sales funnel is a way to map out your customer journey into clear steps. But to build a revenue-generating machine, the key is to overlay data on each step of your customer journey so you can continually improve it.

In this chapter, you will learn how to expand your reach by creating your own revenue-building machine. But before I tell you the details, let me first illustrate it with two stories.

Don't focus on setting sales goals; focus on building a revenue-generating system.

CASE STUDY: DANIELLE LESLIE

I first met Danielle Leslie over ten years ago when she was working as a sales rep for an ad network providing ads to one of my companies. I remember sitting down with her at a coffee shop in San Francisco during one of the conferences, and she told me that her dream was to be an entrepreneur like me and become her own boss. She was young and very ambitious.

Eventually, she quit her job at the ad network company. She joined an online education company that seemed very promising, but it didn't do as well as expected, and she was fired less than six months later. She ended up moving back to her mom's apartment in uptown Oakland, one of the poorer neighborhoods in the San Francisco Bay Area, which was very tough for her.

The good news was that in the six months she spent at this online education company, she learned a lot about online education that most people didn't know. She began putting together an online class that she advertised for $1,990. After platform cost and discounts, it would generate about $1,294 per client on average.

Once she created her course, she began with an advertisement on Facebook like the one you see here.

When people clicked on the ad, they were redirected to a simple one-page website where they could register to attend a free webinar. Out of the people who clicked on the ads, 29 percent registered for the free webinar. That meant over 70 percent of the people who clicked on the ad didn't even register for the free webinar. And out of the people who registered for the free webinar, only 19 percent of them attended the pre-recorded webinar. So 19 percent of the 29 percent attended the webinar.

Just to recap: People saw the ad, clicked on it, saw that the webinar was free, yet only 29 percent of them registered. And then, even with multiple follow-up emails reminding people that the webinar is starting tomorrow, starting in two hours, or starting now, only one person out of five actually showed up to watch the hour-long pre-recorded webinar.

To the people who attend, she makes an offer at the end of the webinar: "If you want to join my online class, it costs $1,990." Two of the people attending the webinar will buy the class and pay the $1,990.

After the webinar, she has another sequence of emails and SMS, and for some of them, a sales call. After the webinar, thanks mostly to the email follow-up, of the 19 percent of the 29 percent of the people who saw the Facebook ads, 3 percent buy the class. That means she makes around 45 percent of her sales during the automated pre-recorded webinar (where she is not physically present) and 55 percent after the webinar from the follow-up email sequence, which is also automated.

Those engagement numbers may not look great on the surface. But here are her average numbers per day for the last year or so.

On average per day for the past twelve months, she has spent $35,478 on Facebook ads, with a minimum of $20,000 per day and a maximum of $50,000 per day. As an approximate average, she spent $35,000 on ads on Facebook every day. If you do the math, the average cost per sale—or the Customer Acquisition Cost (CAC)—is $994 per customer.

And while the official price is $1,990, because of the discount and platform fee, on average she makes $1,294 per customer. So that means for every dollar she spent every day on Facebook, she makes 1.3 times that money per customer, or a 27 percent net margin.

Every day for the last 12 months, she's been making $46,000 in revenue, or $12,000 in profit per day. On a yearly basis, it's around $16 million in revenue, or $4.4 million after the cost of the ads.

Her course is fully optimized and pre-recorded, meaning she only shows up on average once a month. She has two full-time employees doing ads on Facebook, but she pays them mostly on commission based on user acquisition. Otherwise, she's a one-person company.

It sounds like a pretty good sales machine after all, doesn't it? One person is making $46,000 a day, or $15,000 in net profit per day. And others are doing even better. If you are curious about online education, this is the model to follow.

CASE STUDY: RUSSELL BRUNSON

Another great model comes from an entrepreneur I work with named Russell Brunson. Russell wrote a book and advertised it on Facebook. The ad could be summarized as follows: "Hey, if you want to get my book, you can get it for free; just come to my website and register. You'll only pay for the shipping cost, which is about $7. You can buy it on Amazon for $30, or you can get it free here." If you get it free, the only thing Russell asks is you pay for the shipping cost. He doesn't make any money from the shipping cost; it's the real shipping cost.

If you put in your credit card number to pay the $7 shipping cost, he doesn't make any money, but your credit card is now in the system. Then he will make you an offer—it's called a *bump sale*—where you still have the option to pay $7 for the shipping cost and get the book for free, and that's fine. But if you pay $37, you're going to get A, B, and C along with the book. Twenty percent of the people who put in their credit card will end up ticking the box to get the bump sale for $37.

You may think you're finished, but just as you're about to close the window, you have another offer—a *one-time offer*—for $97. Nine percent of the people who enter their credit card number will buy the $97 one-time offer.

Now you may really think you're finished, but then you have a thank-you video to watch. At the end of the thank-you video, Russell offers a second one-time offer that costs $297. This more expensive one-time offer registers you as a member with access to software he developed to go along with the book. Of the people who first put their credit card number in to pay the $7 shipping fee, 4.19 percent end up buying the $297 offer.

If you do the math, on average it costs him $23 to get people from Facebook to his website. Sounds like a lot to give someone a free book, right? But because he has this sales machine combined with the offer, he makes on average $37 per customer.

That's 1.6 times the amount he spends on ads per customer every day. For every $1 put into the machine, he makes $1.60, and he's spending way more than $35,000 on average per day. In fact, Russell built up a full business around this system that is now generating well over $100 million a year. (See the Click-Funnels case study in Chapter 6.)

CREATE YOUR PEAK SALES MACHINE

Okay, so what did we see illustrated in these two stories?

Danielle's and Russell's revenue-generating system has two key ingredients: the core product and a positive economic equation between lifetime value and customer acquisition cost (CAC). Danielle's was 1.3, and Russell's was 1.6.

The Positive Economic Equation

As mentioned in the previous chapter, you have good unit economics when you can recoup your CAC within six months and generate three times your CAC in 18 months. If you're in the gaming or tech industry, it's even better if you can find a profitable way for your cost per install (CPI) to be 10x cheaper than the next competitor.

And once you have the right numbers, like a ratio of 1.3 to 1.6, then you scale up. Scaling up means you can start increasing your advertising spending to $1,000 a day, $5,000 a day, $10,000 a day, $50,000 a day and so forth, depending on your business.

To create your revenue-generating machine, the basic idea is to map out your customer journey, visualize that customer journey as a step-by-step funnel, measure what happens at each step of the funnel, and continually improve.

This is what we call the Atomic Scaling peak sales machine. Here is one example of what this process might look like in practice.

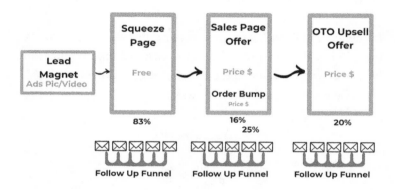

Here we have a four-step funnel, which would work well for a one-person company like Danielle Leslie's. You can have as many steps as you want, but it's best to start simple.

To create your sales funnel and measure at every step, you don't need to develop any software. Any number of software platforms on the market can do this for you, such as Funnelytics, Auto Response, Get Response, 2Tango, and Autogrowth. Most of the software is free to start, because, of course, freemium is the best business model. Depending on how many users you have, you will eventually need to pay on a monthly basis.

The funnel basically starts with a lead magnet—something of value you provide for free. You might run an advertisement on Facebook, with a video or image, and you say, "I'm going to give you something for free." Not something uninteresting, but something that is actually valuable to your users.

Do you remember the core principle from the Revenue chapter? To receive more, you need to give more. If you want to make more money, give more to more people. At this point, the most important thing is not how much money you will make on the bump sale, for example, but getting as many people as possible into your funnel. That means your lead magnet needs to be a good one. It must offer a lot of value to your customers.

Then you need to add value with every step and overlay it with data so you can continually improve.

Once you can do this, you will find your way to 1.3x or 1.6x.

No matter how many steps you have in your funnel, every funnel begins with traffic and ends with follow-up.

So if you use the four-step funnel above, your peak sales machine would have six components:

1. Traffic
2. Lead magnet
3. Squeeze page
4. Sales offer with bump offer
5. One-time upsell offer
6. Follow-up funnel

The traffic starts the engine, and the follow-up funnel brings the magic.

EARN YOUR OBE IN TRAFFIC

Once you've created your sales machine, it's time to test it. To test it, you have to start the engine—you have to get traffic flowing through it.

Too many people believe that if you build a great product, customers will come, but unfortunately that's not the case. It's very common in the start-up world to see companies invest every penny they have in their product. They believe so much in their amazing product that they don't do any marketing. Obviously, the product fails miserably. So while you need to be obsessed with your products, it's probably even more important to be obsessed with your customers. Traffic is just another word for your customers, or users.

You're likely familiar with the Order of the British Empire, otherwise called the OBE. The Order of the British Empire is a nomination that can be made for a professional achievement, business success, or outstanding personal expertise that demonstrates a positive impact and influence on others.

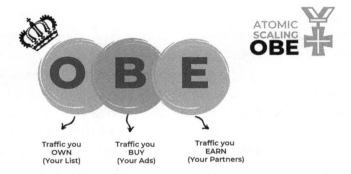

Traffic you OWN (Your List)   Traffic you BUY (Your Ads)   Traffic you EARN (Your Partners)

In the context of Atomic Scaling, OBE means to *Own*, to *Buy*, or to *Earn*. There are three commonly identified ways to get traffic on the internet:

1. Your Own list
2. Buying traffic with ads
3. Earning traffic, typically through partnerships

OWN TRAFFIC

You can receive an OBE nomination for how well you manage your *own* list, meaning your retention numbers are through the roof. Perhaps you have virtually no customer churn from year to year. In that case, like Riot Games (see Chapter 6), you may not need to be very good at acquiring new traffic; you just need to continue delivering outstanding services and new offers to your community, and your revenue-generating machine will roar to life.

CASE STUDY: TCGPLAYER

Chedy Hampson, founder of TCGplayer, worked at a twenty-four-hour sports card shop and a comic book store in the US when the game Magic: The Gathering was released to the public. Magic: The Gathering is a game loosely based on Dungeons & Dragons that is played with collectible cards, which you use to have battles between magicians, wizards, creatures, and so on. Hasbro, the company that owns Magic: The Gathering, has produced over twenty billion Magic cards. And there are over twenty million active players spending a lot of money to buy these cards.

Through his job at the comic book store, and from playing the games professionally, Chedy realized that the point-of-sale system available didn't help manage all the different buying and selling price points for the cards printed. So he launched a content website that eventually included live pricing data to help solve this pain point. This website evolved into an online marketplace with an inventory management suite of tools that used the freemium model and allowed sellers to upload their inventory for free. A successful sale resulted in a charge of approximately a 10 percent transaction fee.

The TCGplayer marketplace quickly grew into a full-fledged platform that rivaled eBay and Amazon within the collectible card gaming space, and now they're generating well over $100 million in revenue. Notice that Chedy didn't technically own the list of comic book store owners, but by creating the software system, he had access to the list. Remember access is part of the BRAW framework for your ideal users. In this case, access to the list is pretty much the same as owning it.

Nearly every collectible card sold in the US goes into his system.

He ended up dominating the category without facing any competition. If you have access to a list and can create a product that serves these people, this list becomes your own list, and you can end up dominating the market without any competition, just like Chedy. Other larger online marketplace companies quickly noticed, and in 2022, Chedy received an offer from eBay to acquire TCGplayer for $295 million.

BUY TRAFFIC

You can also receive an OBE nomination for how well you *buy* traffic. You may be good at buying traffic from Google, LinkedIn, TikTok, YouTube, or your local newspaper, but most likely you have mastered the art of ads acquisition on Facebook, which is where most of the traffic is right now. You can grab the attention of potential customers within seconds and get them to join your own list.

If you would like to be OBE-nominated for buying traffic, especially on Facebook, you will need to know who your competition is. Do you know the number one industry category buying ads on Facebook, representing close to 50 percent of Facebook's ad revenue? The gaming industry. When anyone buys an ad on Facebook, there's a 50 percent chance they are fighting for the same user attention as a game company. Out of every two ads you see on Facebook, one of them is from a gaming company. If you're ready to pay $1 for a user, and a game company can pay $1.1 for the same user, which ad is Facebook going to be showing to the user? The gaming ad.

The gaming industry is powerful enough to buy 50 percent of the traffic on Facebook, the biggest platform for ads. So, if you want to acquire users, you have to be able to beat the game industry.

Here's an example of an outlier who did just that—a company called Voodoo.

Voodoo, a French hyper-casual gaming company, has been ranked the 4th mobile app publisher by number of downloads only behind Facebook (Facebook, Instagram, WhatsApp), Google (Chrome, Gmail, YouTube), and Bytedance (TikTok), with nearly five billion downloads (see case study in Prediction chapter).

The average length for a game ad on Facebook is 15 seconds. Voodoo looked at all the data from their ads, and they realized that 80 percent of the clicks on their Facebook ads happened in the first three seconds.

You can learn from Voodoo's data too. If you are creating a Facebook ad, ask yourself if people get what you do in the first three seconds. If you review a video ad from your team, your marketing agency, or your marketing team member, pay attention to the first three seconds. Discuss the storyboard for the first three seconds. It doesn't matter what happens at seconds 4, 5, 6, 7, 8, 9, 10, 11, 12, 13, 14, and 15 because 80 percent of the people will not even see it.

You may wonder, *If it's just three seconds, why not just use text?* Video may be more expensive, but it has a better return. If you do run an ad with photo and text, like Danielle Leslie's, the photo is the most important, and be sure not to use too much text. Whether it's video, text, or a photo, if people don't get what you're doing within three seconds, then your ad is probably not very good.

You can test it for yourself. You may not have 5 billion downloads to prove it, but I'm sure you've noticed that everyone's attention span is quite short right now. If you don't get the attention of people very quickly—within the first three seconds—you're probably not going to get clicks.

EARN TRAFFIC

You can also get an OBE nomination for how well you *earn* traffic—nourishing partnerships and communities that serve similar audiences to yours. We'll call you the king or queen of partnerships.

You don't have to create traffic; it's already there. You just need to find where your people are. There is a template I love called the Dream 100. It's attributed to the late Chet Holmes, author of *The Ultimate Sales Machine* and former salesperson for investor Charlie Munger. Your Dream 100 includes your top one hundred dream clients. According to Holmes, "The goal of the Dream 100 is to take your ideal buyers from 'I've never heard of this company' to 'What is this company I keep hearing about?' to 'I think I've heard of that company' to 'Yes, I've heard of that company' to 'Yes, I do business with that company.'"[59]

In his book *Traffic Secrets*, Russell Brunson applies this concept to traffic sources, where your Dream 100 includes the top one hundred influencers, companies, or media outlets your dream customers or buyers currently follow. The idea is to gradually and authentically connect with each of your Dream 100 to turn them into your fans, endorsers, and referral partners—so they will naturally promote you to their communities, which happen to include your ideal customers.[60]

Rovio, the creator of Angry Birds, almost never did paid advertising, yet the game has over five billion downloads. That's because Rovio's founder, Peter Vesterbacka, deserves an OBE nomination for his capability to sign partnerships. His partnerships include Star Wars, McDonald's, NASA, National Geographic, the singer Shakira, and the United Nations.

Eighty percent of ad clicks happen in the first three seconds.

Peter's energy and enthusiasm are contagious. Angry Birds had a pretty good list to begin with, but Peter is still the ultimate fisher of partnerships—I've seen him in action myself. No matter who Peter meets, he will start to preach and try to convert that person into a partner.

You don't need to create a community. You can just piggyback on existing ones.

They were able to sign these high-value partnerships because Peter is good at preaching, but also because the team delivers. Delivering quality for previous partners made it easier for Peter to preach and convert. It's a virtuous circle. So to earn traffic through partnerships, you need to be the king or queen of preaching, but you also need to make sure that your team overdelivers and makes everyone look good.

If you master the capability of retaining and managing your own list, of buying traffic, and of earning traffic, you will not only be nominated as an OBE, but also excel in the game of business. If you are an OBE master, you are a very scarce resource. There are not many people like you in any industry. If you have an OBE master in your company, make sure to cherish them like your own child.

Now is your time to shine and get OBE-nominated for generating traffic for your business!

THE MAGIC IS IN THE FOLLOW-UP FUNNEL

Once you get the engine of your sales machine going, remember that the magic isn't just in the steps of your sales funnel. It's in the follow-up funnel.

If you have a lot of live events, sales, and special offers in your industry, like we do in the gaming industry, you have to have the discipline not only to follow up, but to track your engagement. It may be through SMS, WhatsApp, or something else, but you need to have the discipline to track it. I'll discuss this more in the next chapter on retention.

Here is an example of how I have used the follow-up funnel personally. In one of my recent workshops, my goal was to reach an 80 percent engagement rate for my workshops, which is quite high. I track the engagement rate every day, and by the end of the week, I could pretty much predict what the engagement rate would be by Sunday night at 11:59—and I was worried we would not reach 80 percent.

Two hours before 11:59 on Sunday, I sent a reminder that people could still submit their workbook. I don't usually do that, but I did it that night because I knew that if I did not do it, we would not reach the 80 percent goal. As a result, I received enough submissions to reach exactly 80 percent. In this case, my follow-up funnel was a simple message two hours before the workshop, which increased the engagement rate to 80 percent.

For a recent webinar, I was similarly concerned I would not hit an 80 percent engagement rate, so I included pictures of the Nintendo Switch in my follow-up email. Everybody knows what a Nintendo Switch looks like, but I used pictures because they have a better effect on my engagement rate than words. Some people respond best to words, while others respond best to pictures. How did I know the pictures increased my engagement rate? Because I tracked it.

In your follow-up funnel, every step should be tracked, and every action should have a purpose. You don't send five emails for the sake of sending five emails. You send five emails because you know that the first email is going to increase your engagement by X percent, your second email by Y percent, and the third email by Z percent. You know that if you don't send a reminder for people to join a live webinar one hour before, 30 minutes before, and 5 minutes before, you might lose 20 percent of your attendees.

You don't need to create a community. You can just piggyback on existing ones.

In the case of Danielle, everything she's doing is optimized, and she makes 16 million a year as a one-person company. She is able to do this because she tracks everything. For example, 19 percent of the people who respond to her Facebook ad attend her webinar. If she doesn't send the follow-up email between the time the people register and the time they attend, that number drops to 5 percent. But because she sends an email, she gets 19 percent. Others, like Russell, use SMS for this kind of funnel, and their rate is much higher than 19 percent.

What if you don't have any data yet, and you're introducing a new program to customers? Is there a rule of thumb for the follow-up funnel? How much is enough—and too much?

There is no rule of thumb per se, but five is a good target. If you only have one reminder, people might not read it. You can find out by tracking the opening rate for your message yourself. A 20 or 30 percent open rate is generally considered pretty good. That means if you only send one message, for 70 percent of the people, it's like you never sent a message.

As a general rule, and as long as it doesn't hurt your engagement, go ahead and send one more reminder!

How many messages you send is important, but when you send the message is probably even more important. For example, Russell always sends a message two hours before, 30 minutes before, and even five minutes before. Again, people have a very short attention span. If you don't send them a message five minutes before joining the call, they may forget the call they booked two days ago. Not everyone uses calendars and reminders on their phones. (See the Retention chapter for more on engagement and re-engagement.)

Here is your Atomic Scaling ultimate sales machine at a glance:

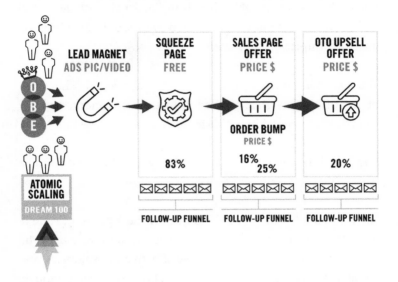

Remember, what you can visualize, you can measure, and what you can measure, you can improve. Once you have a positive ROI, where your LTV to CAC ratio is higher than 1, automate and scale as much as you can. The reason why Danielle spends $35,000 a day is because she cannot spend more than $35,000 a day without seeing her metrics decrease. Otherwise, she would spend $350,000 a day.

And even if Danielle didn't have $350,000 a day to spend, there are services that would be happy to give her $350,000 a day, and she could pay them back a month or more later. As long as you can show that these kinds of machines are in place, people trust these numbers because all this is trackable and clear.

Anyone who has the technical capability to create this kind of funnel can scale to these numbers. You don't have to have

$35,000 to spend each day. Remember, Danielle was living in one of the poorest neighborhoods in California with her mom, and she didn't have any money when she started. Just visualize, measure, improve, and scale.

You also don't need your own data to get started. There are plenty of services that provide industry benchmarks to help you to create a good hypothesis, such as App Annie.

And if you feel you are not reaching your objective for any reason, just focus on how you can give more.

Once you are tracking your leads, know the amount of time it takes from lead capture to sale to revenue, and have hit your positive LTV to CAC ratio, you have effectively developed a predictable revenue-generating machine. But reach is not enough for Atomic Scaling. Ultimately, the most important metric is *retention*. If you have very low churn, it almost doesn't matter how much it costs to acquire users or how much you charge—as we will see in the next chapter.

GAME ON: REACH

- ☐ Earn your OBE in traffic.
  - ○ **Own traffic.** How will you reach out to your own list?
  - ○ **Buy traffic.** How will you optimize your ads on your chosen platform?
  - ○ **Earn traffic.** Who are your Dream 100 traffic sources? How can you reverse engineer your Dream 100 into partnerships?
- ☐ **Create your peak sales machine.** What steps will you include in your sales funnel? Are you building a model you can test?

- ☐ **Bring the magic with your follow-up funnel.** What follow-up sequence will you use for each step in your funnel?
- ☐ **Measure, iterate, and scale.**
  - ○ Are you overlaying each part of your funnel with data? For example, are you creating your hypotheses? Are you measuring? And are you making changes based on the data you received?
  - ○ What is your CAC versus LTV ratio? If you don't have numbers yet, what do you want them to be?

Chapter 6

RETENTION

"Don't let your customers quit."

—NICOLO LAURENT, CEO OF RIOT GAMES

I was having lunch with Nicolo Laurent, early employee and now CEO of Riot Games, in his office in Santa Monica. He had just launched League of Legends, and things were okay, but not amazing. His investors were putting a lot of pressure on them to get a lot more users and a lot more revenue. At the time, the easiest way to grow your reach and revenue was to buy advertising on the equivalent of Facebook (in this case, it was MySpace and Google) and hope that you would get your money back within a certain number of weeks or months, just like we talked about in the previous chapter on Reach.

But it wasn't working for them. About 60 percent of their users were coming from YouTube, specifically from streamers who were doing videos about the games. But ads, including ads on YouTube, weren't converting profitably or at scale.

What would you do if you were the CEO at Riot? Well, Nicolo, along with the two founders, Brandon Beck and Marc Merrill, decided that if they were terrible at reach and terrible at revenue, they were going to be the best in the world at retention. Then Nicolo literally spent the next two hours explaining to me exactly how he was going to do that.

For example, League of Legends is all about belonging to a clan. If you're not part of a clan, the game is tough to play, and you're likely to quit. The community was competitive, which didn't always bring out the best in everyone. Some players were insulting and downright toxic, and these players regularly got kicked out of clans for bad behavior.

Someone at Riot Games who was crunching data realized that if a player got kicked out of a clan and didn't join a new clan within two weeks, they would likely leave the game and never return. Now, what would you do if your most obnoxious customers voluntarily left your organization? I think most people would say, Good riddance!

Well, Nicolo is not most people, and in the data he found his competitive advantage. He saw an opportunity to make Riot Games the best in the world at customer retention by making League of Legends the stickiest game on the market. How did Riot do this?

They made sure that every player who got kicked out of a clan got at least three invites to a new clan within two weeks. If those clans didn't work out, you might think those players were just too toxic to bother with. But that's not how you create the stickiest game on earth.

The game makers found a way to take the people who were too toxic to fit in any other clan and put them all in their own clan together—and they loved it! The players realized—okay, we're all together because we're all the bad guys, and actually it's kind of fun to be all together. And they would eventually learn to get along and stop insulting each other.

This intention to "never let your customer quit" made League of Legends the stickiest game on earth, and Riot Games the best in the world at customer retention.

Unfortunately, that wasn't enough for their investors. To them, Riot Games was growing too slowly, mainly because they could never find a profitable customer acquisition model. The initial investors sold Riot Games to Tencent for $420 million, and they thought they had made the deal of a lifetime. One of these investors was Mitch Lasky, legendary investor at the Silicon Valley venture capital firm Benchmark, former entrepreneur and video game executive, and originally founder at Jamdat, which was sold to Electronic Arts.

Within a few years of being acquired by Tencent, League of Legends was generating $20 *billion* in revenue.

What did Tencent see in Riot Games that the initial investors missed? Tencent understood the competitive advantage of customer retention and was more than happy to turn their $350 million investment into billions of dollars.

Most investors, CEOs, and sales reps focus on reach and revenue as signs of growth, but out of the three Rs—reach, retention, and revenue—retention is potentially the most profitable. In fact, if you are really good at customer retention, it is possible to be terrible at reach and revenue and still have an incredibly profitable business.

RETENTION IS THE HOLY GRAIL OF BUSINESS

"Your business model has monetization happening after the download, so your users need to be around for long enough to be monetized."

—MIKE MORAN, HEAD OF GROWTH AT USERWISE

Why is retention so powerful? In freemium businesses, monetization happens after (and sometimes quite a while after) the initial download and activation. So if you don't retain, you don't monetize—it's as simple as that.

Also, it's a lot less expensive to re-engage existing users versus acquiring new ones—in fact, it's about five times cheaper. The second purchase of an existing user usually tends to be a lot higher and happens faster than the first-time purchase. It's commonly known that a 5 percent increase in customer retention can increase profits anywhere from 25 to 95 percent.

What separates a good company from a great company is not the flamboyant CEO gathering new crowds on stage, always launching new products and expanding into new territories. The best businesses I know are nothing like that. They rely on relationships and trust and then develop loyalty with their customers—customers that will follow them wherever they go.

Just like Riot, Rovio, the maker of Angry Birds, was never able to acquire users through Facebook. As of now, they still don't know how to buy users on Facebook. It's too expensive for them. But they don't care. Angry Birds has generated billions of dollars in lifetime revenue, and Rovio's first Angry Birds movie alone made over $350 million. Their retention is so good that their customers stick around forever.

Think about your own company. Are you focused on acquiring users, or are you more focused on monthly recurring revenue (MRR)? MRR—or even better, annual recurring revenue (ARR)— is the retention metric to focus on.

What are you focusing on?

New Customer   **ARR**

In the Reach chapter, we talked about shifting from hunting to fishing and from setting goals to creating a system. Retention is about shifting from wild fishing to farm fishing. It might be more fun to fish in the wild, but you can do better business as a farm fisherman. Farm fishermen know where the fish are and make sure they constantly reproduce and grow. It's the same for a business focused on retention: they deliver far better results than those focused on reach alone.

Retention is also about shifting from setting goals to creating a system. If the freemium revenue model is about getting users to stick around, retention is about getting users to stick around for as long as possible. So instead of setting fast revenue and user acquisition goals, in this chapter you'll learn how to create a system that makes your customers want to stick around forever—otherwise known as a LOVE machine.

CASE STUDY: CLICKFUNNELS

ClickFunnels, a SaaS (software as a service) company based in Boise, Idaho, is pretty much playing by the book when it comes to Atomic Scaling.

ClickFunnels allows you to create a webpage that functions as a sales funnel and online store, all without having to hire a technical team. Many companies were doing something equivalent before ClickFunnels, and you can do the same on WordPress, Shopify, and similar platforms. Yet ClickFunnels has been growing very, very fast.

For example, ClickFunnels reached $100 million in revenue in the first five years without a penny from outside investment, being fully funded by the founders Russell Brunson (see his case study in Chapter 5) and Todd Dickerson, and by sales. They have a small team and only three salespeople in the whole company: the CEO plus two others. In terms of sales, everything else is automated.

Their business is very simple: they have one software product, ClickFunnels, that they sell with two plans, the basic plan and the platinum plan. With the basic plan, you have a limited set of features, and with platinum, you have more features. The basic plan is $97 per month, which is already quite pricey for

SaaS websites, and the platinum plan is $297 per month. If you pay for a year in advance, the monthly price drops to $247. Currently, the monthly recurring revenue (MRR) is $118, which means most people have the basic plan and gradually upgrade to platinum.

What's magical about ClickFunnels is they have over 95 percent year-on-year retention, the holy grail metric for SaaS businesses.

The business is all about upselling, whether it's from the free trial to $97 per month or $97 to $297 per month. Some customers are spending $25,000, $50,000, and even $100,000. How is this possible when their core product is $97 or $297 per month?

The answer is through selling services. For the last three years, in addition to their core software product, they've been running weekly five-day live events (most of which are automated), monthly twenty-one-day and thirty-day challenges, and one yearly offline event for the community. For this year's event, they booked Universal Studios, an entertainment park in the United States, for three days and welcomed 3,000 people in person and tens of thousands of people streaming online.

This year they're most likely going to reach 200 million dollars in revenue, representing 1.8 billion contacts aggregated, as their customers have their own customers on the platform.

Most of their revenue today (70 percent) is from software, and 30 percent is from services, which consist of the events they have organized over the last three years.

Most users are acquired through online training, and once

people are in their funnel through online training, then they upsell the software.

ClickFunnels typically gets traffic from Facebook ads, where they offer a free workshop on setting up your own online business as a small and medium enterprise, for example. The first hour is training, and the last 30 minutes is upselling to join the next workshop at around $100. They barely mention their software.

Once you sign up for the next workshop, they quickly upsell you to other services that can range from $25,000 to a full-day consulting service for $100,000 per day. These higher-end services aren't their core business; they're very happy to sell you the training and the software.

ClickFunnels also has affiliated businesses. Every customer of ClickFunnels by default has their affiliate numbers in a very prominent position on their dashboard. If you share a link with a friend and the friend registers, your affiliate numbers go up and you earn a percentage.

One of the reasons why ClickFunnels has only three salespeople (including the CEO) yet earns hundreds of millions of dollars of revenue is because they have a very strong affiliate network.

The result is that ClickFunnels has well over a 50 percent net margin. Not only do they have a high customer retention rate, they also have a high employee retention rate. When they're making $200 million in revenue with $100 million-plus in profit and have no investors, that means every month they're making $10 million in profit for their small team. All the employees are very well paid for people who are based in Idaho, which means they are also very loyal.

BUILD A LOVE MACHINE

Approximately 92 percent of the gaming industry's revenue on PC and mobile is generated by the freemium model. Even with hundreds of games launching every week, games like Candy Crush, Clash Royale, Pokemon, and others are still able to maintain top-grossing status, making billions of dollars per year, consistently year over year.

"League of Legends succeeded not because of our ability to attract new customers. It was our ability to retain them."

—MARC MERRILL, CO-FOUNDER OF RIOT GAMES

These developers have mastered the art of retention. Specifically, they have mastered a *system* that has allowed them to own the audience's attention long enough to build up their community and ultimately generate revenue. This is true for gaming companies as well as SaaS businesses like ClickFunnels.

In the gaming industry, that system is called *LiveOps*. Other industries might call it live operation, or live services. Broadly speaking, LiveOps includes updates, announcements, and new content for the product, all data-driven to increase retention and ultimately increase revenue.

LiveOps includes anything not integral to user functionality and the core product. For example, ClickFunnels' core product is building a simple website to sell a product. Their training and events are their LiveOps.

Most traditional companies have sales and marketing people dedicated to finding new customers, and product development people dedicated to the core product. But they typically don't have anyone dedicated to improving the product and serving their existing customers better.

The reason gaming and software companies are so good at the game of LiveOps is because they've been accumulating billions of data points and using them to optimize the customer experience. In comparison, studies show less than 20 percent of companies overall even track customer retention rigorously.

For example, Electronic Arts used to be a very traditional business, mostly selling physical products in supermarkets. Then, when Andrew Wilson became the CEO, they began to focus on LiveOps. Soon they had 50-plus percent of their revenue from LiveOps. As of 2022, they announced that 70 percent of their $5 billion yearly revenue comes from LiveOps.

That means most of their revenue comes from existing games where they just work the machine of retention—which is a lot less like work and a lot more like playing a game. In fact, the user acquisition numbers for most of their products are decreasing. Yet their revenue and profit have never been higher.

"Live Ops does not necessarily guarantee downloads. What it ensures is that if you get some traction with your game, you're able to more safely and predictably turn that into a sustainable business."

—SIMON HADE, CEO OF SPACE APE GAMES

So how can a company have a decreasing customer base and fewer new products released year over year and yet have more revenue and profit than they ever have?

They build a retention machine consisting of live product development, organized event calendars, strong sales, and offers based on billions of data points, reducing churn as much as possible.

ATOMIC SCALING LOVE MACHINE

ENGAGEMENT
and Re-Engagement
Automation

LIVE
Product
Development

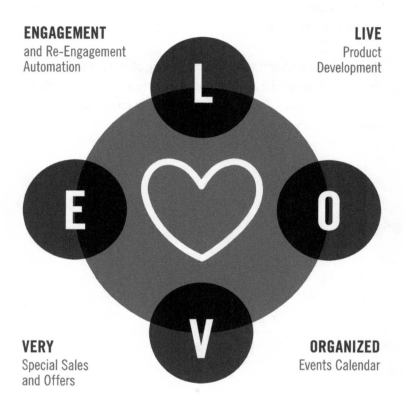

VERY
Special Sales
and Offers

ORGANIZED
Events Calendar

L _____ Product Development

O _____ Events Calendar

V _____ Special Sales and Offers

E _____ and Re-Engagement Automation

In fact, you need what I call a LOVE machine. LOVE stands for

- Live product development
- Organized event calendars
- Very special sales and offers
- Engagement and re-engagement

The LOVE machine provides love for your community. It's ultimately about providing the best service to your users to keep them coming back again and again. It's a system for building retention into the DNA of your business.

LIVE PRODUCT DEVELOPMENT

Live product development is very similar to the concept of Lean Startup or Agile. You launch your product fairly early, you collect data points from users, and you keep improving the product based on user feedback.

You will have two types of data points: one driven by analytics, and the other driven by the vocal users in your community. One is left-brained, numbers driven, and analytical. The other is more right-brained and story based, which helps develop your community.

In this first stage of building your LOVE machine, you are developing your product DNA. Your playbook and the freemium revenue model can help you come up with your initial hypothesis for your product DNA. You'll be answering questions like, Is my product going to be sticky? Can it generate a good business? If you're collecting data, you'll be able to answer these questions from the very first version of your product.

For example, Voodoo is typically looking for 40 percent retention after day one. That means from the people who install the app today, they expect 60 percent of the people not to come back tomorrow. In other words, they are expecting 60 percent churn. After seven days, it's typically 15 percent retention. After 28 days, it's around 6.5 percent retention. On average, people will play for fifteen minutes per session, and during these fifteen minutes, ads will be shown from time to time, typically in between sessions.

If they have a game that meets these metrics, based on other data they have collected, they can be 80 percent sure they will make at least a million dollars within one week of launching the game.

Voodoo tracks these early retention metrics from version one through version five. If the product has more than five iterations, they usually kill the product. If a game has low retention from the start, they also usually kill the product. For example, if version one's retention is 10 percent when they were expecting 40 percent, there is no need to bother with versions two, three, or four. They just kill the game and start another one.

On the other hand, if their day one retention is 50 percent, and if their day seven retention is 15 or 20 percent, they will probably be getting excited and think, *Wow, this is huge—this is going to be a hit.* Then they will check the other metrics, and usually six to eight weeks later, they will launch the game and have an 80 percent chance of making at least $1 million in one week.

This is Voodoo's process for live product development, and they are a master at it. This is why they have over 5 billion downloads and are ranked number three worldwide in downloads on iOS and Android after Facebook and Google, and before Tencent. They have adopted the agile "fail fast, win fast" mindset. They develop quickly, test the retention metrics quickly, and iterate quickly.

So for live product development, here are a few principles.

Build retention into your product DNA. Your product DNA ultimately comes from your playbook and your revenue model (ideally freemium). But people often have a hard time understanding that retention is also part of your product DNA, whether you realize it or not. Just like it's hard to add monetization to your product DNA later, if you have very poor retention from the start, it's difficult to have high retention in the future.

Think of a baby. If a baby has strong DNA at birth, this baby will likely grow up healthy. If the baby has weak DNA, the baby may still be healthy in the future, but it will take more effort—they may need a special diet or supplements, for example. If your product has poor retention DNA, you may end up doing events and sales in the future, but they will likely be cosmetic, so they won't necessarily change and improve the core product.

For your company, what initial metrics will you use to measure the strength of your company's product retention DNA?

Monitor user feedback. If you have quickly launched the first version of your product but you're not monitoring user feedback, you're not doing live product development. In fact, you have the worst of both worlds. Rather than fully following the lean start-up approach of launching, gathering user data, and changing quickly to improve quickly, you've stopped at the first step—with an incomplete product that will likely satisfy no one.

How will your company monitor user feedback?

Make sure your user feedback is not changing your product or user DNA (unless you want it to). As you begin to offer your product to your initial users, you may discover that what you thought was the right way to develop the product might be very different from what your user feedback and data are saying. That's why the initial user set is so important—you want to make sure you're actually serving who you want to serve.

For example, one SaaS business I am working with is doing very well; they have more customers than they can handle, and they're growing very fast. They also keep hiring salespeople, who keep bringing in more customers.

They began with a very specific product DNA. Now many customers are saying they're ready to pay hundreds of thousands or millions of dollars for it right now, and because they want to catch all the fish in the ocean, suddenly the product roadmap is first come, first serve—meaning they will add whatever features their new large customers want.

The problem is that the customers who are first in line are driving the DNA of the product, but they have nothing to do with the mission of the company. Their feedback is changing the DNA of the product because they're not a fit with the users who the company originally wanted to serve.

This might be fine for a year or two, but after three years, the company might wake up with a product that has nothing to do with what they originally wanted to do or why they wanted to do it. Sometimes this is okay, but you have to be intentional.

In the case of this company, we created a waiting list for the customers who have nothing to do with the DNA of the product. We'll still serve them, but not now. We will first serve the customers who fit with what the firm is trying to achieve.

Make sure you are able to make the changes from your user feedback. This may seem obvious, but it's worth pointing out. If you are collecting feedback from your community that you know will make your product stickier, that's great, but if it takes you three or four months to make those changes, that's not so great.

When it comes to product iteration, the speed of iteration is almost more important than the actual changes you prioritize. If you are not sure what to prioritize or believe you might not have the resources to change based on your customer feedback (customers can be both demanding and creative in their requests!), then the best thing to do is to set a rhythm and adjust the outcomes of each product iteration from these regular releases. That might help you to focus on what matters, just like Daniel Ek at Spotify did when he was prioritizing early catalog depth and buffering time!

Set a product release rhythm. Just as a rhythm is important for your culture (see Chapter 3), it's also important for your product releases. Even more important than the what, the who, and the why of live product development is the *when*. When you do your updates is actually more important than the updates themselves.

As we said in Chapter 3, establishing a rhythm is a lot like going to the gym, or doing yoga. It's far better to go to the gym or your yoga session for three terrible sessions a week than to have one amazing session every two months.

A good rule of thumb for your product release rhythm is to release something new every four to six weeks. If you're not used to releasing new features regularly, that may sound ridiculously difficult—how can you release something new every four weeks? Even if you have three minor releases in a row, if you stick with it, a few months later it will seem easy and your releases will improve. You won't question it; you'll just be doing it.

ORGANIZED EVENT CALENDARS

While your product is being developed, you can compensate for what your product is not doing yet with a regular rhythm of events for your community.

To create this rhythm, start with an editorial calendar. What is an editorial calendar? An editorial calendar lists all the events you are planning for the year and when they will occur. They typically align with offline events.

You can start with significant events or holidays in your country. For example, you might list Christmas, New Year's, Valentine's Day, Halloween, Chinese New Year, Independence Day, National Day, or Election Day. Any kind of holiday or event that is big in your country offline is a good opportunity to do something online.

Then you can look at internal events, such as the anniversary of your product. In the case of one of my first game companies, one of our big events was when we reached one million Facebook fans. We knew when we were likely to reach one million Facebook fans because we were tracking how many new fans we got per day. But we created an opportunity to increase the pace of new fans by saying when we reach one million fans, we'll have a big party. Suddenly everybody was inviting their friends, because they wanted to be part of this big party.

But even more important than offline events or internal events are your content releases, as you will see in the case of Smilegate.

CASE STUDY: SMILEGATE

The game CrossFire was developed by a Korean company called Smilegate. The founder of Smilegate, HyukBin Kwon, is now one of the five richest people in Korea and the youngest billionaire in Seoul. He started out as an engineer and made all his money through this one game, CrossFire. How did he go from being a regular engineer to one of the richest people in Korea?

HyukBin founded Smilegate in 2002, and when he developed CrossFire, he didn't have much funding. At the time, Korean developers were mostly targeting Korea, Japan, or the United States, which meant they were doing very advanced graphics. HyukBin not only didn't have much of a budget for high-end graphics, he didn't have much of a budget for marketing. So instead of going for the big guys, he decided to go for the small guys with low-end PCs and lower-quality graphic cards, and still make a fun game. So he began by targeting Southeast Asia.

His approach was not very successful, and his company was in survival mode until they signed a publishing deal with Tencent in China. Back then, Tencent had not yet become the world's largest gaming company, but it did have tons of users via its messaging app QQ (in the days before Messenger, WeChat, and WhatsApp). Yet it couldn't monetize its users. At the same time, all the games made in Korea or the United States couldn't be played in China because Chinese gamers were mostly playing from internet cafés with low-end computers. Only games like CrossFire could run on these computers.

So Tencent and Smilegate started working together on their LOVE machine, and the first thing they focused on was their editorial calendar—and specifically their content releases.

In the case of CrossFire, they were releasing a new game mode every quarter, and they had accumulated lots of data points from many hours of usage. (A new game mode is a significant new feature for the game.). After a while, they noticed that every time they released a new game mode, boom! Every dormant user came back because there was something big and new in the product. Then they figured out that if they released one new map every eight weeks, which created a new environment to learn in, boom! Everyone came back again. At first, everyone was excited, but within six or seven weeks, after they had learned the map, they got bored again. Then, at the eight-week mark, boom! They launched a new map.

They did the same thing by introducing new characters and new weapons, but the impact of the new character or weapon only lasted about six weeks.

Similarly, with cosmetic changes to hair color or clothing, they discovered the impact was only three weeks.

This data determined how they would organize their editorial calendar: Every eight weeks, a new map was scheduled to be released. Every six weeks, a new character or weapon would be released. And every three weeks, a new cosmetic change would be released.

You can create your editorial calendar in stages. For example, if you're not typically releasing new content regularly, you can start with every quarter. Then you can increase to once every two months, then once a month, and so on.

Remember, if you just throw events out there one after the other, but you don't make a hypothesis and you don't measure, you won't learn very fast. You might even wonder if it's really useful to do all these events; they're taking so much time. But if you set a hypothesis and measure how much the event actually impacted your metrics, then you'll quickly find out what's working. You can double down on the events that are working, but for the events that aren't working, you can stop doing them or do them differently.

For your company, do you have an editorial calendar?

What and when are the major events in your calendar, including festivities?

What rhythm are you planning for your content releases?

What exactly will you do for each planned event, and what will it impact?

What tools will you use to monitor the impact of your events?

Remember, if you're not monitoring, you're just working and not improving. Set your hypotheses, measure, and then make changes accordingly.

VERY SPECIAL SALES AND OFFERS

Creating very special sales and offers is another way to give LOVE to your community. As you're considering what special sales and offers to create, consider the following principles.

Know your bestselling product categories in terms of volume and revenue. First, look at what your community already buys most from you—and what produces the most revenue. List your top bestsellers, both in terms of revenue and volume. What products or services are your best sales contributors?

Segment your customers for special sales and offers. Do you have the ability to target specific customer segments? Gaming companies often create what is called a "big guns" offer, which is an event that always outperforms the others. An example from the gaming industry might be a special sniper contest. But to join this contest, you not only have to pay a very high price, you have to use a specific sniper or a specific item in the game. And if you don't have this item and want to be part of this big challenge, you have to buy the item just to be part of the challenge.

For a big guns offer, you can do a target segmentation that

might include all the users who have the item already and all the users you think are on the verge of buying this item. Of course, you will promote the event to those who already have this item because they are all champions. But for all those on the verge of buying the items, you will double down on your communication to give them a very special prize and offer if they buy this item.

What might be your company's big guns offer?

Use a variety of messaging and display capabilities. I often hear, "We're making so many offers, but nothing's happening!" What they may not realize is that only 5 percent of their users are seeing their offer displayed on Facebook—and Facebook is the only place they display their offers. I say 5 percent not by accident; that's actually the average. Gaming companies tend to use forums such as Reddit for their very special offers. If only 5 percent of your people see your offer, because 95 percent of them don't bother to visit your page on Facebook, that means your offer is 95 percent less efficient than what it should be.

Similarly, if you use an automatic message sequence to advertise your offer, be sure you're using the messaging tools your community checks often.

Where do your top users gather? What messaging tools do they use? Be sure to use communication tools your users regularly use.

Use anchoring or other similar techniques for your sales offer. Gaming and SaaS companies also use very specific techniques to optimize sales conversion rates. One technique is called *anchoring.* With anchoring, you don't just make one offer of, for example, $4.99; you make a series of offers before you make the real offer. If you compare the conversion rates of making one offer versus a series of offers, the conversion rate of the series approach is significantly higher than a one-time offer.

How might you use anchoring with your next special sale or offer?

Set a rhythm for your very special events. Just like setting an editorial calendar is important for content releases and regular events, creating a rhythm and flow for your very special offers and events is also important.

Think of your very special events like a symphony. A symphony begins slowly, building anticipation, until you reach a crescendo of excitement. Then there is resolution, and a new movement begins. There is a big difference between offers with no cadence at all and those who are making offers like Beethoven would play a concerto.

You can discover the best times for your crescendos, or your offers, from your buying data. When do the majority of your users make a new purchase? Is it on a Friday? a Monday? a Tuesday?

Let's say it's Friday. That means when you create your sequence of messages (using anchoring, of course), you will probably want that sequence to culminate in your best offer on Friday.

As an example, a game that one of my companies developed, UberStrike, the largest first-person shooter (FPS) on Facebook, was making twice as much revenue on a Friday than it would on a Monday. Saturday and Sunday, on the other hand, generated 30 percent more revenue than an average Tuesday and Thursday. So we would start announcing offers on Tuesday and Thursday while anchoring and expecting peak revenue on Wednesday and Friday. We could predict, with a 5 percent margin of error, our revenue for the next week, based on the kind of offers we were crafting.

What very special sale or offer could you make to your community, and how often?

ENGAGEMENT AND RE-ENGAGEMENT

Remember how Riot manages their churn rate with people who get kicked out of their clans? As Nicolo Laurent said, Don't let your customers quit. Do whatever it takes to have a 95 percent retention rate year over year.

Know the definition of an active user and how to measure it. Knowing when to engage and re-engage begins with clearly defining your active users. For gaming companies, downloading the app does not make you an active user. What is the definition of being active for your company? What metrics do you use to measure whether a user is active or not? Maybe an active user is someone who logs in at least once a day, at least 70 percent of the day throughout any given month, or at least X hours per month.

Know the definition of a dormant user, what typically causes user churn, and how to measure it. Dormant means a user used to be active, and now the user is inactive. How would you define a dormant user for your company? What causes users to become dormant? In the case of Riot, if you get kicked out of a clan, that's nearly a 100 percent guarantee you will be inactive within two weeks if you don't join another clan in the meantime. If you're using the freemium model, can you estimate the conversion rate from active to paying to inactive? This will help not only with retention but with user acquisition.

List the required steps to go from dormant to active. Once a user becomes dormant, what steps can they follow to become active again?

Some companies have a "magic number" for retention. Supercell's magic number is day 30, being around 20 percent. Your magic number depends on your playbook, your business model, the kind of product you offer, and the kind of users you acquire. To discover your magic number, just remember, "What gets measured gets managed." If you keep trying things but don't measure or don't have a clear hypothesis, it's going to be difficult to know what you should do versus what you should not.

As a first hypothesis, begin re-engaging dormant users with a series of five communications. Before we can measure and change, we must start with some kind of hypothesis for re-engagement. Typically what works very well is a five-step re-engagement sequence.

The first message can be a very soft touch, just a check-in to see how they're doing. Then you can offer a series of different offers or events, specifically targeting these users. Usually, you will re-engage a dormant user in step two or step three. If you get to step five and receive no response, you can probably assume this approach is not going to bring this user back. So set a new hypothesis, measure, and keep iterating.

As we learned from Riot and many other gaming companies, re-engaging your dormant users is often the easiest way to grow. Don't let your customers quit!

CASE STUDY: ELECTRONIC ARTS (EA)

In the 2010s, LiveOps didn't exist outside of Asia. LiveOps was invented in South Korea, was mastered in China, and took the rest of the world by storm, including the United States, Europe, Southeast Asia, and so on.

LiveOps came about after the emergence of free-to-play, which first took off in Korea, with virtual and dual currency. At that time, there was a company in the west called Electronic Arts (EA), one of the largest companies in the USA.

By 2013, Electronic Arts was in trouble. They were primarily making money by creating new games and launching them for $69 each.

In the first week, they would generate 50 percent of the game's lifetime revenue. Within the first month, they would generate 90 percent of the game's revenue. Then they constantly had to launch new games and invest a lot in marketing because they made 90 percent of their lifetime revenue in one month, and the majority of that in the first week.

Business was becoming very difficult. Electronic Arts didn't have enough new products to sustain growth, so their revenue overall was declining. The user base was also declining, so their existing games were suffering. The margins of the company were getting pretty tight, as they were also facing a lot of competition from other countries, mostly from Asia and South Korea, when free-to-play emerged.

Meanwhile, marketing was getting more and more expensive, which was already a big part of the company's expenses. Finally, the CEO of Electronic Arts resigned, and for more than six months, the company didn't have a CEO. Can you imagine one of the biggest gaming companies in America and Europe without a CEO for six months? With margins getting tighter and tighter and the revenue and user base continuing to decline, their new product launches were just not enough to sustain them. And the board of Electronic Arts couldn't figure out who could take over the company as CEO.

Andrew Wilson, a younger guy from Australia, had joined Electronic Arts when he was twenty-six years old and was taking care of Asia. From there, he grew EA Sports, a division of Electronic Arts, and became an executive producer for a game called FIFA. At that time, it was FIFA 3.

Even though he was a young guy with limited managerial skills, Wilson pitched the board of EA to consider him as CEO, to leverage what he learned working with Nexon, a big gaming company in Korea that was their commercial partner. Nexon had taken FIFA, the soccer game EA developed, made it freemium, and ran it as a live service. And this business model had produced good results in Korea.

Andrew Wilson pitched to the board of EA, "What if we could

run all our games like Nexon is running our games in South Korea? Even with our user base declining, marketing costs increasing, and being unable to launch new products, what if we could still grow our business revenue and profit using LiveOps?" After six months with no CEO, in September 2013, Andrew Wilson was named CEO of one of the largest gaming companies in the USA. At that time, EA had earned the nickname "dinosaur," because people thought it was going to disappear.

Andrew Wilson stayed true to his promise to learn from the way Nexon operated their games using LiveOps. This meant doing a few things differently:

- Using live product development instead of constantly launching new games
- Having a very strong event calendar
- Coming up with targeted offers
- Segmenting users and creating specific offers for each segment
- Establishing retention as the priority—not user acquisition and not launching new games

As CEO, Wilson began implementing LiveOps practices for all of EA's games. Within ten years, EA's revenue increased by a factor of three. The market cap of EA (inclusive of net margin) increased by a factor of five. Now EA is worth around $40 billion, its highest valuation yet. Out of its $5.7 billion in revenue, 70 percent is from LiveOps.

Andrew Wilson is still one of the youngest CEOs in an American publicly listed company. Last year, his salary and bonus were $67 million. Most importantly, Electronic Arts, once seen as a dinosaur, is now seen as an example and thought leader in live operations. In fact, more than 58 percent of the revenue from gaming companies in the West comes from LiveOps—a significant transformation by any measure.

BUILD A THRIVING COMMUNITY

In this chapter, we've been focusing a lot on numbers and data. But ultimately, the LOVE machine is about heart. The true key to retention is to build a thriving community—to understand the powerful human desire for belonging.

There is much more to building community than the LOVE machine, which is beyond the scope of this book, but the LOVE machine is a very good start to building a community your people will want to be a part of for a long time.

David Spinks is the founder of CMX, a community that helps professional community builders thrive in their work. Spinks previously worked for Loic Le Meur, iconic French entrepreneur and investor in Silicon Valley, community builder and conference organizer, and founder of LeWeb. CMX is now part of the Bevy Group, whose investors include Ryan Smith at Qualtrics. Bevy's founder, Derek Andersen, also founded the startup community StartupGrind and learned the art of community management while at the gaming company Electronic Arts.

Here are the six guiding indicators CMX recommends for getting a new community off the ground and thriving:

1. You don't "launch" a community; you leverage an existing one.
2. People join communities to feel safe and validated.
3. Curate high-quality members to start things off.
4. In-person and live online experiences create stronger bonds.
5. You'll need to manufacture the first interactions.
6. The most essential factor is you.[61]

Whether they realized it or not, founders Brandon Beck and Marc Merrill followed these same six principles as they built a thriving community at Riot Games.

CASE STUDY: RIOT GAMES

Based in Los Angeles, California, Riot Games is a game developer, publisher, and e-sports tournament organizer with twenty-four offices worldwide and over 2,500 staff members. In February 2011, Tencent acquired a majority stake in Riot Games and fully acquired it in December 2015.

Brandon "Ryze" Beck and Marc "Tryndamere" Merrill founded Riot Games after bonding over video games as roommates and business students at the University of Southern California.[62]

Disenchanted with their post-college careers and the business practices of most game developers at the time, who typically did not listen to fans, they built their new company around a free-to-play model where games evolved based on user feedback.

During the first few years, they developed their game League of Legends primarily in response to feedback from online forums.

As a multiplayer online battle arena video game, League of Legends was a freemium game that earned revenue through microtransactions.

In League of Legends, players play as "champions," each with their own abilities that strengthen through gameplay. They compete against other champions, some of which are other players and some of which are computer generated.

In the most common mode of play, two teams of five compete against each other by attempting to destroy the other team's Nexus. Champions use defensive structures called turrets to defend their Nexus, so winning a match involves getting past the other team's turrets and destroying their Nexus. Since the company's creation in September 2006 and its first game, League of Legends, in October 2009, Riot has grossed over twenty billion dollars in revenue. Most of it comes from its flagship product, League of Legends, making it one of the highest-grossing game franchises in history.

Here are a few other League of Legends (LoL) facts:

- It has the largest game footprint in streaming media platforms like YouTube and Twitch.
- It regularly ranks first in hours watched on those same platforms.
- It had nearly eight million peak concurrent users each day as of September 2019.
- The League of Legends World Championship in 2019 had one hundred million unique viewers, peaked at a concurrent viewership of forty-four million, and offered a minimum prize pool of US$2.5 million that featured a collaboration

between Riot Games and world luxury top brand Louis Vuitton.[63]

So how did Riot grow LoL to become one of the highest-grossing game franchises in history with the highest number of concurrent players worldwide?

Two core beliefs formed the foundation of Riot Games:

1. Games would be built based on feedback from the community.
2. Games would constantly evolve through regular content updates and events, based on the "game as a service" model, a concept popularized in Asia but still relatively unheard of in the West at that time.

When Brandon and Marc founded Riot as two recently graduated business students, they already had a strong sense of community. As they developed their company and LoL, they also happened to follow the six best practices identified by CMX, a community that helps professional community builders thrive in their work.[64]

1. Riot didn't "launch" a community but leveraged an existing one.

Beck and Merrill were originally inspired by the game mod Defense of the Ancients (DOTA) for Warcraft III: The Frozen Throne, which had been built by passionate players. When they began developing their own game idea, they piggybacked on this existing community of DOTA players. "DOTA proved that games as a service are something that can work because it grew virally due to the efforts of great creators, a community of moderators, and a community of volunteers with zero advertising dollars spent," Merrill said to the *Washington Post*. "It was just this direct relationship with players and this willingness to evolve and grow the game over time."[65]

2. People join communities to feel safe and validated.

Then Beck and Merrill hosted a DOTA tournament at USC to find these passionate players who knew the mod well. Among them, they met Paul Bellezza and Jeff Jew, both super fans of the original DOTA game. Both ended up becoming the first two interns at Riot.[66]

3. Curate high-quality members to start things off.

Early on, they hired Steve "Guinsoo" Feak, one of the original designers of DOTA Allstars and known for his work on Defense of the Ancients, to help them develop what would later become League of Legends.[67]

4. In-person and live online experiences create stronger bonds.

With their new team in place, they quickly put together a demonstration of the game in about four months for the 2007 Game Developers Conference in San Francisco, one of the gaming industry's key gatherings.[68]

5. You'll need to manufacture the first interactions.

During the first few years, League of Legends developed primarily in response to feedback from online forums.[69] Riot had one of the original designers and some of the top players. Its location was also physically close to Blizzard, in Los Angeles, maker of the game StarCraft, from which DOTA was created. All contributed to Riot's early success.

6. The most essential factor is you.

Riot still maintains its focus on listening to its players, both fans and detractors.

Yet they also know the player isn't always right.

"How do you be player-centric and care about what your customers want but then literally say, 'Well, sometimes they're wrong,'" said Merrill to the *Washington Post*. "It's because to me, players are great at problem identification but often are not great at solutions."

Riot remains dedicated to listening to their players while also cultivating their community long term.

"About 75 percent of our players don't say I play League of Legends. They say I am a League of Legends player," said Merrill. "That's the difference between saying I play golf or I like to surf, and I'm a surfer. It's an identity opt-in designation that relates to a lifestyle, and a mindset, and memes, and this community that people are deeply immersed in."[70]

GAME ON: RETENTION

- ☐ Live product development
  - ○ **Build retention into your product DNA.** What initial metrics will you use to measure the strength of your company's product retention DNA?
  - ○ **Monitor user feedback.** How will your company monitor user feedback?
  - ○ **Make sure your user feedback is not changing your product or user DNA (unless you want it to).** How will you make sure you are prioritizing your BRAW users?
  - ○ **Make sure you are able to make the changes from your user feedback.** What resources do you need to make the changes your users are requesting? If you don't have the resources to make those changes right now, what rhythm will you set to regularly iterate your product based on feedback?
  - ○ **Set a product release rhythm.** How often will you release new versions of your product?
- ☐ Organized event calendars
  - ○ Do you have an editorial calendar?

- What major events will you add to your calendar, including festivities?
- What rhythm are you planning for your content releases?
- What exactly will you do for each planned event, and what will it impact?
- What tools will you use to monitor the impact of your events?

☐ **Very special sales and offers**
- **Know your bestselling product categories in terms of volume and revenue.** What products or services are your best sales contributors?
- **Segment your customers for special sales and offers.** How might you target specific customer segments for your special sales and offers? What is your "big guns" offer?
- **Use a variety of messaging and display capabilities.** Where do your top users gather? What messaging tools do they use?
- **Use anchoring or other techniques for your sales offer.** How can you optimize your sales conversion rate?
- **Set a rhythm for your very special events.** How often will you offer your very special sales and offers?

☐ **Engagement and re-engagement**
- **Know the definition of an active user and how to measure it.** What is the definition of being active for your company? What metrics do you use to measure whether a user is active or not?
- **Know the definition of a dormant user, what typically causes user churn, and how to measure it.** How do you know when a user goes dormant? What typically causes users to go dormant or quit? What metrics do you use to measure whether a user is dormant or not?

- List the required steps to go from dormant to active. Once a user becomes dormant, what steps can they follow to become active again?
- As a first hypothesis, begin re-engaging dormant users with a series of five communications. How can you make sure your customers don't quit? How might you automate this process?

WHAT'S NEXT?

"It doesn't matter if I failed. At least I passed the concept on to others. Even if I don't succeed, someone will succeed."

—JACK MA, FOUNDER OF ALIBABA

In your hands, you have the full blueprint for beginning your journey of Atomic Scaling.

Remember the 3P3R framework:

1. **People:** Hire less, empower more.
2. **Prediction:** Prediction is as important as production.
3. **Playbook:** Create a finite game and play to win.
4. **Revenue:** Offer your basic service for free.
5. **Reach:** Serve the largest total addressable market you can.
6. **Retention:** Retention is more important than reach or revenue.

Right now, you have a chance to be an early adopter of this paradigm shift and create a positive future for more people, whether you are working on your next startup, lead a large company, or head up a government or nonprofit organization.

Acquire these superpowers, and you will outperform those who don't.

As a reminder, here are the action steps for acquiring these superpowers and scaling to serve:

GAME ON: PEOPLE

- ☐ **Think with both sides of your brain.** How might you use storytelling *and* data the next time you're enrolling someone in a task or project?
- ☐ **Stay as small as possible.** Instead of hiring more people, how might you invest in the people and the culture you have to increase performance and profitability?
- ☐ **Focus on team performance, not individual talent.** How might you create a culture of trust and accelerate team performance in your company rather than focusing on individual skills or talent alone?
- ☐ **Focus on magical pairs.** Who are the magical pairs in your company? How might you arrange for them to work together more often if they don't work together already? How might you assemble a team around them?
- ☐ **Hire EPIC employees.**
  - ◦ **Employees.** How might you increase the number of customers each employee serves?
  - ◦ **Profit.** Is your profit scaling higher than your revenue? If not, what one thing might move the needle the fastest?
  - ◦ **Impact.** What is the mission of your organization? Is it more powerful than compensation to your employees?

Do your employees care about your customers—do they want to serve them?

  ◦ **Cost.** How might you take one step toward the Valve 2.5x rule in your organization?

GAME ON: PREDICTION

☐ **Bring the power of prediction to the people.** How might you begin shifting more of your decisions to your team?

☐ **Learn how to predict.** Are you teaching your team how to predict and use mathematical probabilities in their daily work? Are you focusing on the process rather than results?

☐ **Know the difference between prediction and Prophecy.** Do you know the difference between prediction and Prophecy—and when to do both?

☐ **Practice the prediction cycle of hypothesis, measure, change, and repeat.** In what area of your business can you begin practicing the prediction cycle of set a hypothesis, measure, change, repeat?

GAME ON: PLAYBOOK

☐ **Define your mission.** What is your moonshot? What ignites such passion in you and your team that would be worth trying and failing at?

☐ **Define your users with the BRAW Framework.**
  ◦ What big total addressable market can you serve?
  ◦ Who do you relate to?
  ◦ Who do you have access to?
  ◦ Who do you want to serve?
  ◦ What group of people meets all four of these criteria? These are your BRAW users.

☐ **Define your method.** How can you begin using prediction as part of your core method in your company?

☐ **Set a rhythm.** What weekly meeting or activity can you schedule now to provide structure to your company and strengthen your culture?

GAME ON: REVENUE

☐ **Start with purpose.** Remind yourself of your mission and why you are creating this revenue model in the first place.

☐ **Get tons of free users.** What service or product would appeal to the largest number of your users so you can have a big total addressable market?

☐ **Get users to stick around.**

　○ Does your product or service solve a one-time problem, or a recurring problem? If it solves a one-time problem, is there a recurring problem you could solve for your ideal users?

　○ How can you solve your ideal users' recurring problem on a daily or weekly basis?

　○ How can you optimize your session or service time? Are you minimizing download time, if applicable?

　○ If your users must use other products and services to use your product or service, how might you develop those yourself, perhaps through your own ecosystem?

　○ What are the significant profitability and retention benchmarks for your industry, both offline and online? Create a hypothesis and prediction cycle to aim for these benchmarks.

☐ **Create a service or product whose value increases with time.**

　○ How might you leverage the power of inventory, or personal data, in your product or service?

- How might you leverage the power of connections, or the network effect, in your product or service?
- ☐ **Keep cost per user low.** How might you lower your cost per unit, using a dynamic definition of cost?
- ☐ **Get the skills to create the product or service.** What skills do you need to automate, develop, or hire for?
- ☐ **Create a clear monetization plan.**
  - Who are the minnows, dolphins, and whales in your business?
  - How can you monetize your product or service for each of these segments?
  - What are your free versus paid offers? Where are your paywalls?
  - What is your ideal monetization lifecycle and funnel, from free sign-up to activation to first-time purchase to upsell? How do users flow between multiple paid offerings?
  - Are you measuring to know when customer lifetime value is greater than customer acquisition cost (LTV>-CAC)? When LTV>CAC, it's time to scale.

GAME ON: REACH

- ☐ **Earn your OBE in traffic.**
  - **Own traffic.** How will you reach out to your own list?
  - **Buy traffic.** How will you optimize your ads on your chosen platform?
  - **Earn traffic.** Who are your Dream 100 traffic sources? How can you reverse engineer your Dream 100 into partnerships?
- ☐ **Create your peak sales machine.** What steps will you include in your sales funnel? Are you building a model you can test?

- ☐ **Bring the magic with your follow-up funnel.** What follow-up sequence will you use for each step in your funnel?
- ☐ **Measure, iterate, and scale.**
  - ○ Are you overlaying each part of your funnel with data? For example, are you creating your hypotheses? Are you measuring? And are you making changes based on the data you received?
  - ○ What is your CAC versus LTV ratio? If you don't have numbers yet, what do you want them to be?

GAME ON: RETENTION

- ☐ **Live product development**
  - ○ **Build retention into your product DNA.** What initial metrics will you use to measure the strength of your company's product retention DNA?
  - ○ **Monitor user feedback.** How will your company monitor user feedback?
  - ○ **Make sure your user feedback is not changing your product or user DNA (unless you want it to).** How will you make sure you are prioritizing your BRAW users?
  - ○ **Make sure you are able to make the changes from your user feedback.** What resources do you need to make the changes your users are requesting? If you don't have the resources to make those changes right now, what rhythm will you set to regularly iterate your product based on feedback?
  - ○ **Set a product release rhythm.** How often will you release new versions of your product?
- ☐ **Organized event calendars**
  - ○ Do you have an editorial calendar?

- What major events will you add to your calendar, including festivities?
- What rhythm are you planning for your content releases?
- What exactly will you do for each planned event, and what will it impact?
- What tools will you use to monitor the impact of your events?

☐ **Very special sales and offers**
- **Know your bestselling product categories in terms of volume and revenue.** What products or services are your best sales contributors?
- **Segment your customers for special sales and offers.** How might you target specific customer segments for your special sales and offers? What is your "big guns" offer?
- **Use a variety of messaging and display capabilities.** Where do your top users gather? What messaging tools do they use?
- **Use anchoring or other techniques for your sales offer.** How can you optimize your sales conversion rate?
- **Set a rhythm for your very special events.** How often will you offer your very special sales and offers?

☐ **Engagement and re-engagement**
- **Know the definition of an active user and how to measure it.** What is the definition of being active for your company? What metrics do you use to measure whether a user is active or not?
- **Know the definition of a dormant user, what typically causes user churn, and how to measure it.** How do you know when a user goes dormant? What typically causes users to go dormant or quit? What metrics do you use to measure whether a user is dormant or not?

For some of you, these action steps and reflection questions will be all you need to move forward. Perhaps you were able to instantly identify which of the 3Ps and the 3Rs you needed to work on and which step to begin with. If so, great!

Others of you may be thinking, *I need to work on all of them! Should I work on all of them at once? Which ones should I prioritize? What should I do first, second, and third?*

TAKE THE ASSESSMENT

If that sounds like you, go to AtomicScaling.com for a free assessment to discover what type of high-performance leader you are, identify your strengths and challenges, and find out where to start your Atomic Scaling journey.

CREATE YOUR CUSTOM ATOMIC SCALING PLAN

To create your own custom Atomic Scaling plan, return to the action steps and reflection questions for each chapter. Identify which action steps you have completed and which ones you haven't. Put the action steps you haven't completed for each chapter on your business growth to-do list. The reflection questions associated with each action step will help guide you in customizing how to complete each step for your business.

As a high-performance leader, you should have regular time scheduled each week to work on the growth of your business. (If you don't, scheduling this time should be the first item on your to-do list!) Then set a rhythm of working through these action steps during your regularly scheduled business growth time.

Now you have a custom plan for maximizing your strengths and minimizing your challenges as a business leader, and with your new rhythm of working on your business regularly, you have the peace of knowing you're prioritizing the most important tasks for scaling your business.

In addition to the assessment, you'll also find more resources at AtomicScaling.com to support you as you continue to level up, including live trainings and more.

Take action. Join the movement at atomicscaling.com

ABOUT THE AUTHOR

 **LUDOVIC BODIN** is an entrepreneur, investor, and the creator of the 3P3R Method® and Atomic Scaling Framework®.

Over the past decade, he has invested in businesses ranging from gaming companies in California, live streaming entertainment companies in China, a fintech company in Hong Kong, a new hydrogen-powered car, a fan-engagement company in Malta, e-commerce in Shenzhen, an AI Platform as a Service company in Paris, and a longevity company in New York City. Many of his investments have already passed unicorn level, with a valuation superior to one billion dollars.

His mission is to help entrepreneurs, philanthropists, and changemakers apply the Atomic Scaling Framework to their organizations and scale to serve.

Ludovic lives with his wife and two daughters in Beijing, China.

WHO'S WHO IN
ATOMIC SCALING

- Peter Vesterbacka, Co-Founder at Rovio (Angry Birds)
- Ilkka Paananen, Co-Founder and CEO at Supercell
- Kevin Lin, Co-Founder at Twitch
- Ralf Reichert, Co-Founder at ESL

- Touko Tahkokallio, former Game Lead at Supercell and former game designer of Boom Beach and HayDay
- Charles Huang, Co-Founder of Guitar Hero (Activision)
- Shaun Lelacheur Sales, Co-Founder at Cmune
- Nicolo Laurent, former CEO at Riot Games
- Bertrand Schmitt, Co-Founder of Data.ai (AppAnnie)
- Kai-Fu Lee, author of *AI Superpowers*
- Reid Hoffman, Co-Founder of Linkedin, author of *Blitzscaling* and investor in Facebook and Zynga
- Gabe Newell, Co-Founder at Valve Software
- Niklas Zennstrom, Co-Founder at Skype and investor at Atomico
- Richard Branson, Co-Founder at Virgin
- Bill Campbell, author of *The Trillion-Dollar Coach*
- Mikko Kodisoja, Co-founder at Supercell
- Joakim Achrén, Co-Founder at Next Games
- Philip Tetlock, author of *Superforecasting*
- Danny Hernandez, former data scientist at Twitch
- Alexandre Yazdi and Laurent Ritter, Co-Founders at Voodoo
- Andrew Trader, Co-Founder at Zynga
- Mark Pincus, Co-Founder at Zynga
- Roy Sehgal, former VP and GM at Zynga
- Astro Teller, CEO at X (Alphabet's moonshot factory)
- Jeff Weiner, former CEO at LinkedIn
- Russell Brunson, Co-Founder and CEO at ClickFunnels
- Jason Citron, Co-Founder and CEO at Discord
- Min Liang-Tan, Co-Founder and CEO at Razer
- Changpeng Zhao, Co-Founder and former CEO at Binance
- Sheryl Sandberg, former COO at Facebook (Meta)
- Mark Zuckerberg, Co-Founder and CEO at Meta
- Josh Kaufman, author of *The Personal MBA*
- Stewart Butterfield, Co-Founder at Flickr and Slack

- Phil Libin, Co-Founder at Evernote
- Daniel Ek and Martin Lorentzon, Co-Founders at Spotify
- Sean Parker, Co-Founder at Napster
- Fabrice Grinda, Co-Founder at FJ Labs
- James Clear, author of *Atomic Habits*
- Danielle Leslie, Co-Founder at Course from Scratch
- Chedy Hampson, Co-Founder at Tcgplayer
- Chet Holmes, author of *The Ultimate Sales Machine*
- Brandon Beck and Marc Merrill, Co-Founders at Riot Games
- Mitch Lasky, Co-Founder at Jamdat and investor at Benchmark
- Mike Moran, Head of Growth at Userwise
- Todd Dickerson, Co-Founder at ClickFunnels
- Andrew Wilson, CEO at Electronic Arts
- Simon Hade, Co-Founder and CEO at Space Ape Games
- HyukBin Kwon, Co-Founder at Smilegate
- David Spinks, Co-Founder at CMX
- Derek Andersen, Co-Founder at StartupGrind and Bevy
- Jack Ma, Co-Founder at Alibaba
- Henry Fong and James LaLonde, Co-Founders at Yodo1
- Timo Soininen, Co-Founder at Small Giant Games
- Dave McClure, Co-Founder at FBFund and 500StartUps
- Pony Ma, Co-Founder and Chairman at Tencent
- Chris DeWolfe, Co-Founder at Jam City
- Kent Wakeford, Founding COO at Kabam
- Bernard Kim, former President at Zynga and CEO at Match. com
- Frederic Descamps, Co-Founder at Manticore Games
- Joseph Kim, Co-Founder and CEO at Lila Games
- Ouyang Yun, former VP at Tencent and Co-Founder at Asia Innovations Group
- Andy Tian, former CEO at Zynga China and Co-Founder at Asia Innovations Group

FURTHER READING

PEOPLE

Catmull, Ed and Amy Wallace. *Creativity, Inc.: Overcoming the Unseen Forces That Stand in the Way of True Inspiration.* New York: Random House, 2014.

Comaford, Christine. *SmartTribes: How Teams Become Brilliant Together.* New York: Portfolio/Penguin, 2013.

Gil, Elad. *High Growth Handbook: Scaling Startups from 10 to 10,000 People.* San Francisco: Stripe Press, 2018.

Grove, Andrew S. *High Output Management.* New York: Vintage Books, 1995.

Hastings, Reed, and Erin Meyer. *No Rules: Netflix and the Culture of Reinvention.* New York: Penguin Press, 2020.

Horowitz, Ben. *The Hard Thing about Hard Things: Building a Business When There Are No Easy Answers.* New York: HarperBusiness, 2014.

Horowitz, Ben. *What You Do Is Who You Are: How to Create Your Business Culture.* New York: HarperBusiness, 2019.

McCord, Patty. *Powerful: Building a Culture of Freedom and Responsibility.* San Francisco: Silicon Guild, 2018.

Schmidt, Eric, Jonathan Rosenberg, and Alan Eagle. *How Google Works.* New York: Grand Central Publishing, 2017.

Schmidt, Eric, Jonathan Rosenberg, and Alan Eagle. *Trillion Dollar Coach: The Leadership Handbook of Silicon Valley's Bill Campbell.* London, UK: John Murray, 2020.

Scott, Kim. *Radical Candor: Be a Kick-Ass Boss without Losing Your Humanity.* Rev. ed. New York: St. Martin's Press, 2019.

Thiel, Peter and Blake Masters. *Zero to One: Notes on Startups, or How to Build the Future.* New York: Crown Business, 2014.

PLAYBOOK

Clear, James. *Atomic Habits: An Easy & Proven Way to Build Good Habits & Break Bad Ones.* New York: Avery, 2018.

Harnish, Verne. *Scaling Up: How a Few Companies Make It...and Why the Rest Don't.* Ashburn, VA: Gazelles Inc., 2014.

Hoffman, Reid and Chris Yeh. *Blitzscaling: The Lightning-Fast Path to Building Massively Valuable Companies.* New York: Currency, 2018

Hoffman, Reid, June Cohen, and Deron Triff. *Masters of Scale: Surprising Truths from the World's Most Successful Entrepreneurs.* New York: Currency, 2021.

Ries, Eric. *The Lean Startup: How Today's Entrepreneurs Use Continuous Innovation to Create Radically Successful Businesses.* New York: Crown Business, 2011.

Sculley, John. *Moonshot! Game-Changing Strategies to Build Billion-Dollar Businesses.* New York: RosettaBooks, 2014.

Sinek, Simon. *Start with Why: How Great Leaders Inspire Everyone to Take Action*. New York: Portfolio/Penguin, 2009.

Sinek, Simon. *The Infinite Game*. New York: Portfolio/Penguin, 2019.

Tse, Edward. *China's Disruptors: How Alibaba, Xiaomi, Tencent, and Other Companies are Changing the Rules of Business*. New York: Portfolio/Penguin, 2015.

PREDICTION

Doerr, John and Larry Page. *Measure What Matters: OKRs: The Simple Idea that Drives 10x Growth*. Portfolio/Penguin, 2018.

Lee, Kai-Fu. *AI Superpowers: China, Silicon Valley, and the New World Order*. Boston: Mariner Books, 2018.

Tetlock, Philip E. and Dan Gardner. *Superforecasting: The Art and Science of Prediction*. New York: Crown, 2015.

REACH

Brunson, Russel. *Traffic Secrets: The Underground Playbook for Filling Your Websites and Funnels with Your Dream Customers*. Carlsbad, CA: Hay House Business, 2020.

Bacon, Jono. *The Art of Community: Building the New Age of Participation*. 2nd ed. Sebastopol, CA: O'Reilly Media, 2012.

Blanchard, Ken and Sheldon Bowles. *Raving Fans: A Revolutionary Approach to Customer Service*. New York: William Morrow and Company, 1993.

Diamandis, Peter H., and Steven Kotler. *The Future Is Faster Than You Think: How Converging Technologies Are Transforming Business, Industries, and Our Lives*. New York: Simon & Schuster, 2020.

Hauge, Michael and Christopher Vogler. *The Hero's 2 Journeys*. Read by authors. Dripping Springs, TX: Writer's AudioShop, 2004. 3 hr., 15 min.

Hoffer, Eric. *The True Believer: Thoughts on the Nature of Mass Movements.* New York: HarperCollins, 2011.

Holmes, Chet. *The Ultimate Sales Machine: Turbocharge Your Business with Relentless Focus on 12 Key Strategies.* New York: Portfolio/Penguin, 2008. Retention.

Jenkins, Henry. *Participatory Culture: Interviews.* Cambridge, UK: Polity Press, 2019.

Kim, Amy Jo. *Community Building on the Web: Secret Strategies for Successful Online Communities.* Berkeley: Peachpit Press, 2000.

Kraut, Robert E. and Paul Resnick. *Building Successful Online Communities: Evidence-Based Social Design.* Cambridge, MA: MIT Press, 2012.

McGonigal, Jane. *Reality Is Broken: Why Games Make Us Better and How They Can Change the World.* New York: Penguin Books, 2011.

Vogl, Charles H. *The Art of Community: Seven Principles for Belonging.* Oakland, CA: Berrett-Koehler, 2016.

RETENTION

Chou, Yu-kai. *Actionable Gamification: Beyond Points, Badges, and Leaderboards.* Milpitas, CA: Octalysis Media, 2015.

Koster, Raph. *A Theory of Fun for Game Design.* 2nd ed. Sebastopol, CA: O'Reilly Media, 2013.

Zichermann, Gabe and Joselin Linder. *The Gamification Revolution: How Leaders Leverage Game Mechanics to Crush the Competition.* New York: McGraw-Hill, 2013.

Lazzaro, Nicole. *Why We Play Games: Four Keys to More Emotion in Player Experiences.* XEODesign, 2004. https://ubm-twvideo01.s3.amazonaws.com/01/vault/gdc04/slides/why_we_play_games.pdf.

NOTES

1   Pagan Kennedy, "William Gibson's Future Is Now," *New York Times*, January 13, 2012, https://www. nytimes.com/2012/01/15/books/review/distrust-that-particular-flavor-by-william-gibson-book-review. html.

2   Tim Sullivan, "Blitzscaling," *Harvard Business Review*, April 2016, https://hbr.org/2016/04/blitzscaling.

3   "How FJ Labs Evaluates Startups," Fabrice Grinda, March 16, 2021, https://fabricegrinda.com/ how-fj-labs-evaluates-startups/.

4   *Merriam-Webster*, s.v. "emotion (*n.*)," accessed April 13, 2023, https://www.merriam-webster.com/ dictionary/emotion.

5   "How FJ Labs Evaluates Startups," Fabrice Grinda.

6   Eric Schmidt, Jonathan Rosenberg, and Alan Eagle, *Trillion Dollar Coach: The Leadership Handbook of Silicon Valley's Bill Campbell* (London, UK: John Murray, 2020).

7   Ilkka Paananen, "10 Learnings from 10 Years," May 13, 2020, Supercell, https://supercell.com/en/ news/10-learnings-10-years/7436/.

8   Simon Sinek, "Performance vs. Trust," 2019, YouTube video, 2:27, https://www.youtube.com/ watch?v=PT09e3ILmms.

9   Sinek, "Performance vs. Trust."

10 Anneken Tappe, "A Record Number of Americans Quit Their Jobs in 2021," CNN Business, February 1, 2022, https://www.cnn.com/2022/02/01/economy/us-job-openings-quite-december/index.html.

11 Paananen, "10 Learnings from 10 Years."

12 Paananen, "10 Learnings from 10 Years."

13 Adapted from Joakim Achren, "Magical Pairs in Game Development," Elite Game Developers, May 25, 2020, https://elitegamedevelopers.com/magical-pairs/.

14 Christine Comaford, *SmartTribes: How Teams Become Brilliant Together* (New York: Portfolio / Penguin, 2013).

15 Paananen, "10 Learnings from 10 Years."

16 Paananen, "10 Learnings from 10 Years."

17 Gabe Newell, "Reflections of a Video Game Maker," The LBJ School, January 31, 2013, YouTube video, 1:02:52, https://www.youtube.com/watch?v=t8QEOBgLBQU.

18 Paananen, "10 Learnings from 10 Years."

19 Paananen, "10 Learnings from 10 Years."

20 Danny Hernandez, "How Our Company Learned to Make Better Predictions about Everything," *Harvard Business Review*, May 15, 2017, https://hbr.org/2017/05/how-our-company-learned-to-make-better-predictions-about-everything.

21 Hernandez, "How Our Company Learned."

22 Philip E. Tetlock and Dan Gardner, *Superforecasting: The Art and Science of Prediction* (New York: Crown, 2015), 69.

23 Tetlock and Gardner, *Superforecasting*, 69.

24 Tetlock and Gardner, *Superforecasting*, 71.

25 Aisha Malik, "Take-Two Completes $12.7B Acquisition of Mobile Games Giant Zynga," TechCrunch, May 23, 2022, https://techcrunch.com/2022/05/23/take-two-completes-acquisition-of-mobile-games-giant-zynga/.

26 Alicia Shiu, "Zynga Analytics at Its Peak," *Amplitude Blog*, June 24, 2015, https://amplitude.com/blog/zynga-analytics-at-its-peak/.

27 Shiu, "Zynga Analytics at Its Peak."

28 Shiu, "Zynga Analytics at Its Peak."

29 Will Dowell, "5 Things We Learned during the Reddit AMA with Gabe Newell," GameSkinny, January 19, 2017, https://www.gameskinny.com/k38nv/5-things-we-learned-during-the-reddit-ama-with-gabe-newell.

30 Zameena Mejia, "Steve Jobs: Here's What Most People Get Wrong about Focus," CNBC, October 2, 2018, https://www.cnbc.com/2018/10/02/steve-jobs-heres-what-most-people-get-wrong-about-focus.html.

31 Marcel Schwantes, "Warren Buffett Says This 1 Simple Habit Separates Successful People from Everyone Else," *Inc.*, January 18, 2018, https://www.inc.com/marcel-schwantes/warren-buffett-says-this-is-1-simple-habit-that-separates-successful-people-from-everyone-else.html.

32 Justine Musk, reply to "Will I become a billionaire if I am determined to be one and put in the necessary work required?," Quora, last updated April 20, 2015, https://www.quora.com/Will-I-become-a-billionaire-if-I-am-determined-to-be-one-and-put-in-the-necessary-work-required.

33 John Naisbitt and Doris Naisbitt, *China's Megatrends: The 8 Pillars of a New Society* (New York: HarperBusiness, 2010), 4.

34 Seth Faison, "Deng Xiaoping Is Dead at 92; Architect of Modern China," *New York Times*, February 20, 1997, https://www.nytimes.com/1997/02/20/world/deng-xiaoping-is-dead-at-92-architect-of-modern-china.html.

35 "Moonshot Thinking," X, accessed April 13, 2023, https://x.company/moonshot/.

36 Astro Teller, "Google X Head on Moonshots: 10X Is Easier Than 10 Percent," opinion, *WIRED*, February 11, 2013, https://www.wired.com/2013/02/moonshots-matter-heres-how-to-make-them-happen/.

37 Teller, "Google X Head on Moonshots."

38 Martin Ramsay, "The Merlin Technique," *Notes from the Woodshed: The Video Blog of Martin Ramsay*, February 10, 2014, http://www.notesfromthewoodshed.com/files/the_merlin_technique.html. See also Jeffrey K. Pinto et al., *Project Leadership: From Theory to Practice* (Newton Square, PA: Project Management Institute, 1998) and Luke Hohmann, *Innovation Games: Creating Breakthrough Products through Collaborative Play* (Upper Saddle River, NJ: Addison-Wesley Professional, 2006).

39 Jessica Conditt, "Angry Birds Series Pecks Up 2 Billion Downloads," Yahoo!, January 22, 2014, https://www.yahoo.com/now/2014-01-22-angry-birds-series-pecks-up-2-billion-downloads.html.

40 Dave Smith, "'Angry Birds' Is the Most Downloaded Game All-Time," *International Business Times*, November 2, 2011, https://www.ibtimes.com/angry-birds-most-downloaded-game-all-time-364390#.

41 Stuart Dredge, "Angry Birds' Mighty Eagle: 'We Have Expanded the Market for Games'," *Apps Blog*, *The Guardian*, March 1, 2012, https://www.theguardian.com/technology/appsblog/2012/mar/01/angry-birds-peter-vesterbacka-rovio.

42 Conditt, "Angry Birds Series Pecks Up 2 Billion Downloads."

43 Conditt, "Angry Birds Series Pecks Up 2 Billion Downloads."

44 Dredge, "Angry Birds' Mighty Eagle."

45 Elizabeth Braw, "Angry Birds Creator Peter Vesterbacka: 'Games Are Good for Your Brain'," *The Blog*, *HuffPost*, March 28, 2012, https://www.huffpost.com/entry/angry-birds-activity-park_b_1384537.

46 Holger Roonemaa, "He Built an Empire from Angry Birds. Now He Wants to Go Underground—Literally," BuzzFeed News, January 17, 2018, https://www.buzzfeednews.com/article/holgerroonemaa/he-built-an-empire-from-angry-birds-now-he-wants-to-go#.thRJlvOjN.

47 Excerpted with permission from Russell Brunson, *Expert Secrets: The Underground Playbook for Creating a Mass Movement of People Who Will Pay for Your Advice* (New York: Morgan James Publishing, 2017), 28–29, 31.

48 Wikipedia, "Valve Corporation," *Wikipedia: The Free Encyclopedia*, https://en.wikipedia.org/wiki/Valve_Corporation, accessed August 6, 2022.

49 Valve Corporation, *Valve: Handbook for New Employees*, 1st ed. (Bellevue, WA: Valve Press, 2012), https://cdn.cloudflare.steamstatic.com/apps/valve/Valve_NewEmployeeHandbook.pdf.

50 Paananen, "10 Learnings from 10 Years."

51 Josh Kaufman, *The Personal MBA: Master the Art of Business*, 10th anniversary ed. (New York: Portfolio / Penguin, 2020).

52 Josh Kaufman, "What Are the '4 Methods to Increase Revenue'?," The Personal MBA, accessed April 13, 2023, https://personalmba.com/4-methods-to-increase-revenue/.

53 "About Evernote," Evernote, accessed April 13, 2023, https://evernote.com/about-us.

54 Wikipedia, "Discord," *Wikipedia: The Free Encyclopedia*, https://en.wikipedia.org/wiki/Discord, accessed August 7, 2022.

55 Wikipedia, "Slack Technologies," *Wikipedia: The Free Encyclopedia*, https://en.wikipedia.org/wiki/
Slack_Technologies, accessed August 7, 2022.

56 Wikipedia, "Stewart Butterfield," *Wikipedia: The Free Encyclopedia*, https://en.wikipedia.org/wiki/
Stewart_Butterfield, accessed August 7, 2022.

57 Gabe Newell, "Reflections of a Video Game Maker," The LBJ School, January 31, 2013, YouTube video,
1:02:52, https://www.youtube.com/watch?v=t8QEOBgLBQU.

58 James Clear, *Atomic Habits: An Easy & Proven Way to Build Good Habits & Break Bad Ones* (New York:
Avery, 2018), 154.

59 Chet Holmes, *The Ultimate Sales Machine: Turbocharge Your Business with Relentless Focus on 12 Key
Strategies* (New Yor: Portfolio / Penguin, 2008), 103.

60 Russell Brunson, *Traffic Secrets: The Underground Playbook for Filling Your Websites and Funnels with
Your Dream Customers* (Carlsbad, CA: Hay House Business, 2020).

61 David Spinks, "How to Build a New Community from Scratch," *CMX Blog*, September 28, 2016, https://
cmxhub.com/how-build-new-community/.

62 "Riot Games," Wikimedia Foundation, Last modified April 19, 2023, https://en.wikipedia.org/wiki/
Riot_Games.

63 Jared Ramsey, "League of Legends Esports 101: Beginner's Guide, Overview, and FAQ," Lineups, July
28, 2020, https://www.lineups.com/esports/league-of-legends/.

64 Spinks, "How to Build a New Community from Scratch."

65 Brian Crecente, "League of Legends Is Now 10 Years Old. This Is the Story of Its Birth,"
Washington Post, October 27, 2019, https://www.washingtonpost.com/video-games/2019/10/27/
league-legends-is-now-years-old-this-is-story-its-birth/.

66 Crecente, "League of Legends Is Now 10 Years Old."

67 Crecente, "League of Legends Is Now 10 Years Old."; "League of Legends," Wikimedia Foundation,
Last modified April 10, 2023, https://en.wikipedia.org/wiki/League_of_Legends.

68 Crecente, "League of Legends Is Now 10 Years Old."

69 "League of Legends," Wikimedia Foundation, Last modified April 10, 2023, https://en.wikipedia.org/
wiki/League_of_Legends.

70 Crecente, "League of Legends Is Now 10 Years Old."

Printed in the USA
CPSIA information can be obtained
at www.ICGtesting.com
LVHW041053290324
775823LV00005B/132/J